DE GRUYTER

OLGA KOKSHAGINA
ALLEN ALEXANDER

THE RADICAL INNOVATION PLAYBOOK

A practical guide for harnessing new,
novel or game-changing breakthroughs

**DE
G**

TABLE OF CONTENTS

DOWNLOAD

Worksheets marked with this
icon can be downloaded here:

▷ **www.degruyter.com/books/9783110641295**

FOREWORD

Most innovation most of the time is about incremental change, doing what we do but a little better. Plenty of studies of technological learning point to the importance of crawling slowly up the performance curve, getting the bugs out and enabling the system to perform with greater productivity. Similarly, market development is a process of improving understanding and meeting needs through incremental upgrades and improvements. The overall economic progress of a wide variety of sectors as diverse as petroleum refining and maize cropping owes a great deal to this systematic incremental process. Continuous improvement of this kind attaches to any product, process or service; it underpins key waves of innovation management thinking like "total quality management", "business process improvement" and "lean thinking".

Incremental innovation is popular not least because it is, to a large extent, manageable. The innovation process is one fraught with risk and uncertainty; creating value from ideas is not the easy task; the "lightbulb moment" as the cartoons often suggest. Taking small steps minimises those risks because we are building on an established foundation and accumulating a knowledge base which we can convert to value in systematic incremental fashion.

The limitation of course is that we can only go so far along incremental improvement curves before diminishing returns set in. And there is the accompanying risk that if we focus too closely on incremental change, we may miss developments elsewhere which allow a competitor or new entrant to challenge us through some form of radical innovation. So any organisation looking to survive and grow needs to build capability for managing this kind of innovation as well.

Innovation history involves a pattern of "punctuated equilibrium" in which for long periods a particular configuration of technology and market will be the "dominant design" with incremental innovation moving it slowly forward in terms of performance. But occasionally a radical alternative emerges which changes the rules of the game – often (but not always) displacing the existing players in the process. And so innovation management needs to build the strategic capability in any organization, public or private, to manage both kinds of innovation.

Definitions of "radical" are notoriously slippery but Richard Leifer and colleagues (in a book of the same name published in the 1990s) made a good stab at it, arguing that the label should attach to innovations which offer some combination of:

○ *totally new performance features*

○ *performance or feature improvement at least five times greater than current*

○ *significant reduction in cost, at least by 30 %*

Clearly such innovations are not just more of the same but with a few improvements along an established trajectory. Instead they will involve doing something different – and they will only happen through taking a different approach to searching, selecting and implementing them to create value.

And it is here that the trouble often starts – because the structures and behaviours needed to support incremental "do what we do better" innovation differ markedly from those needed to enable radical, "do different" innovation. It's not sufficient simply to adopt prescriptions to "think like an entrepreneur" or insert a new department with the role of being the source of internal "start-up" thinking. The risks in radical innovation mean that without a strategic approach organisations can quickly burn through money and time without anything to show for it. Even getting to launch is no indicator of success; there is still the challenge of making and growing a market for whom the innovation may be a long way from what they are expecting.

That's where a book like this becomes valuable. It is not an analysis or a discussion of the nature of radical innovation but rather a how-to-do-it manual, a workbook with advice and guidance for managers seeking to create a capability for working with radical innovation. It builds particularly on business model thinking because those models provide the architecture through which radical new ideas can create value. It's not going to happen through luck or some magical process – and if the architecture is poorly designed there's no guarantee that the whole edifice won't come crashing down at some future stage. So building a strong business model for radical innovation lies at the heart of this book.

It has another very helpful contribution to offer. Innovation is never easy and one the challenges in an organisation with a strong tradition of incremental "safe bet" innovation is that radical ideas (and those who champion them) are often seen as a threat. Machiavelli knew this five hundred years ago and his words are still relevant today:

> *"It must be considered that there is*
> *nothing more difficult to carry out nor more*
> *doubtful of success nor more dangerous*
> *to handle than to initiate a new order*
> *of things; for the reformer has enemies*
> *in all those who profit by the old order,*
> *and only lukewarm defenders in all those*
> *who would profit by the new order".*
> MACHIAVELLI, THE PRINCE, 1532

Olga and Allen usefully address this question head-on, offering not only useful design principles for the value-creating architecture of radical innovation but also some helpful guidance on how to steer a course through the rocky cultural waters of the rest of the organisation.

There's never a guarantee of success with innovation – but we do have enough accumulated experience to be able to learn from the misfortunes of others and to codify their experience into recipes which might help us in our own ventures. This book does a great job of doing that.

PROF. JOHN BESSANT
Chair in Innovation and Entrepreneurship,
University of Exeter

PART 1

ORGANISING FOR RADICAL INNOVATION – WHY BOTHER?

CHAP

INTRODUCTION

This chapter is all about how this book can help you. We assembled useful and thought-provoking content that will help you collect and analyse as much information as you need to substantiate your decisions to launch (or not!). The aim of this playbook is to help managers and innovators make the key decisions about their new, novel and breakthrough ideas.

INNOVATION IS ALL
ABOUT MAKING DECISIONS.

Innovation remains a major concern for senior executives working in today's companies. For instance, a study[1] carried out in 2018 as part of PWC's Global Innovation research suggested innovation was the primary focus of 70 % of company senior executives. An earlier survey involving more than 80 international companies indicated that executives expect their revenue to double every five years thanks to breakthrough innovations[2]. Yet the same survey confirmed almost 90 % of them are unsatisfied with their own innovation efforts.

Innovation is all about making decisions – and making decisions in the corporate context is always challenging. When uncertainty is high and companies face risks of market disruption, it becomes even more challenging. For small companies there are a host of external factors that can and will affect the decision-making process; for large and multinational companies there are just as many external and often more internal factors that will affect the same decisions.

What we aim to do in our playbook is to *help managers and innovators make decisions about their new, novel and breakthrough ideas* by considering not only the innovations themselves (which can be challenging

1 INNOVATION
STUDY
PWC (2018). *The
global innovation
1000 study.*

2 BREAKTHROUGH
INNOVATIONS
Arthur D. Little (2015).
*Systemizing break-
through innovation.*

enough) but also by considering the potential each innovation offers at key decision points during the development stages; setting these against the various organisational structures and operational configurations available to help discover, explore and accelerate their more radical innovations.

Now let's be clear – this book does not aim to be all things to everyone. And to be clear, when we talk of radical innovation, we include those innovations that are by their nature new, either to the company launching them, or to the world. Whilst being new, they may or may not have features that classify them as being novel, but they are most likely to offer some form of a challenge in as much as their newness or novelty requires an element of planned market penetration. Likewise, these new or novel offerings are likely to yield the owners a predicted multiplier of five-times that of their current offerings.

But all this depends on the markets and the behaviour of customers and consumers, so again, *for clarity* we are not considering if, or indeed how, they will breakthrough and/or become adopted, nor are we attempting to predict if they might be disruptive. We think it best to leave that to other knowledgeable scholars on the finer points of diffusion [3] and disruption [4]. Likewise,

3 DIFFUSION OF INNOVATION

To understand how innovations diffuse you can't go far wrong with Everett Rogers's *The diffusion of innovation.* (Rogers, E. M. (2010). *Diffusion of innovations.* Simon and Schuster.

4 DISRUPTIVE INNOVATION

Christensen, C. M. (2013). *The innovator's dilemma: When new technologies cause great firms to fail.* Harvard Business Review Press.

RADICAL INNOVATION – WE INCLUDE THE INNOVATIONS THAT ARE NEW… NOVEL… AND ARE LIKELY TO YIELD FIVE TIMES THAT OF CURRENT OFFERINGS.

we suggest if you are looking for a process-oriented innovation guide[5] or wisdom on the many aspects of managing innovation and entrepreneurship – then we suggest the author of our FOREWORD, Professor John Bessant and his extensive collection of literature will not leave you wanting.

What we are about is providing you useful and thought-provoking content that will help you collect and analyse as much information as you need to sub-stantiate your decisions to launch (or not!).

Therefore, we hope it works for you:

○ *if you are a first-time innovator looking for guidance and help in understanding how you might take your fledgling ideas forward;*

○ *a senior manager looking to invest in and devise your next generation corporate innovation portfolio;*

○ *or you need to tailor your organisational structures to explore and deliver successful innovations.*

And we hope, most of all, that you will enjoy our book – picking it up and putting it down, as your understand-ing of your ideas and innovations increases. We want our book to enable you to realise the potential in your ideas or the ideas of your employees, in your own cor-porate context – whether that be a micro-company, SME or large multinational.

In the spirit of *helping with that navigation,* in Chapter II (of Part 1) we will flesh out the corporate in-novation agenda and begin to explore our take on the various structural models we can see across the world that are aimed at bringing forward new, novel and more radical innovations.

Part 2 of this book then gets far more practical – with recipes for success presented in Chapter II, where we start our innovation journey by outlining the options for both process configurations and organisational structures to set you up for discovery, exploration and preparing for take-off (Chapter III). Once you know what is in the-art-of-the-possible you will have the opportu-nity to explore your ideas or aspirations based on how well you know your possible target markets, contrasted against whether your organisation has the necessary technical skills, manufacturing capability or expertise

[5] **STAGE-GATE PROCESS**

For stage-gate models read:

Robert Cooper (Cooper, R. G. (2001). *Winning at new products: Accelerat-ing the process from idea to launch.*).

required to take your innovations into production (in Chapter IV). These questions will guide you to work-sheets (which we refer to as canvases) exploring these dimensions and *suggesting relative structural configurations that might be beneficial*. What we also hope is that our canvases will help you realise what it is you know, and how to seek out what you don't, by hopping back and forth in Chapters V *(discovery)*, VI *(exploration)* and VII *(prepare for take-off)*, as your knowledge and confidence grows. Once done, not only do we hope you have the *confidence and skills to launch your innovation* but also that you can *build a structure in your organisation that enables you to grow your innovations on a continuous basis*.

Again though, what we must be clear about is our in-ability to build, nurture and reap rewards from your corporate innovation culture. Whilst the right structure will make this activity far less tortuous, this piece of the puzzle is in your hands if you lead the team – remember *"Culture Eats Strategy for Breakfast"*[6] and you need to develop habits and routines to support the culture of your company and focus it toward innovation. We will touch on the cultural dimensions again in Part 3, but for now let's look at the commercial context. «

6 CONSIDERING CULTURE

Accredited to Peter Drucker, but made famous by various other high profile CEOs including Mark Fields, the then-president at the Ford motor vehicle company.

CANVASES WILL HELP YOU REALISE WHAT YOU ALREADY KNOW AND EVEN MORE IMPORTANTLY WHAT YOU DON'T!

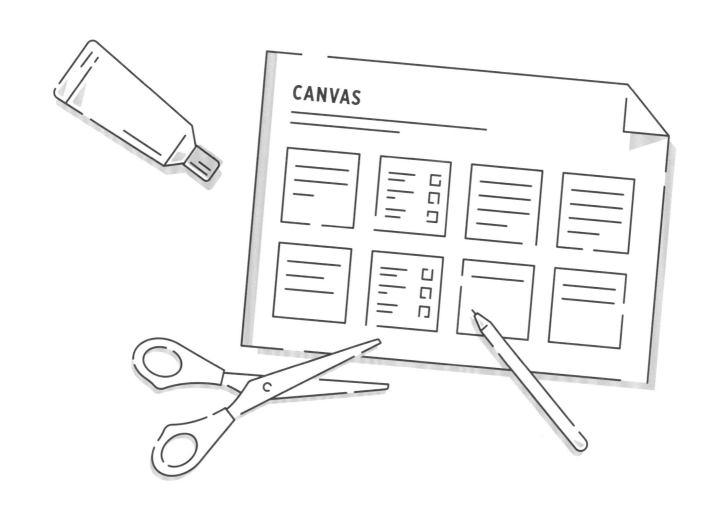

CHAP

SETTING THE CORPORATE INNOVATION AGENDA

This chapter will flesh out the corporate innovation agenda and begin to explore our take on the various structural models we can see across the world that are aimed at bringing forward new, novel and more radical innovations. Our goal here is to help you navigate our book.

**INNOVATION – IT IS ABOUT
GROWING THE REVENUE "CAKE"!**

E stablished organisations around the world are constantly seeking solutions to develop and improve their offerings and to create growth potential from innovation – by growing the revenue "cake" rather than continuously pursuing operational and supply-efficiencies to protect their profit margins (simply sustaining the "cake").

Likewise, the early to mid-term development phases of a new company formation can be chaotic as they work to stabilise operations, chase down cost efficiencies whilst ensuring orders are fulfilled effectively and reliably.

The dilemma in both of these instances is trying to balance the tensions between efficiency of operation (just-in-time procurement, inventory control, lean manufacturing processes and speedy supply) whilst also considering the effectiveness of operations (supplier reliability, production quality, sales force management, accurate delivery and warranty).

However, the challenge does not end there – as for many companies their market share is being eroded by competitors, or technology is moving on and leaving

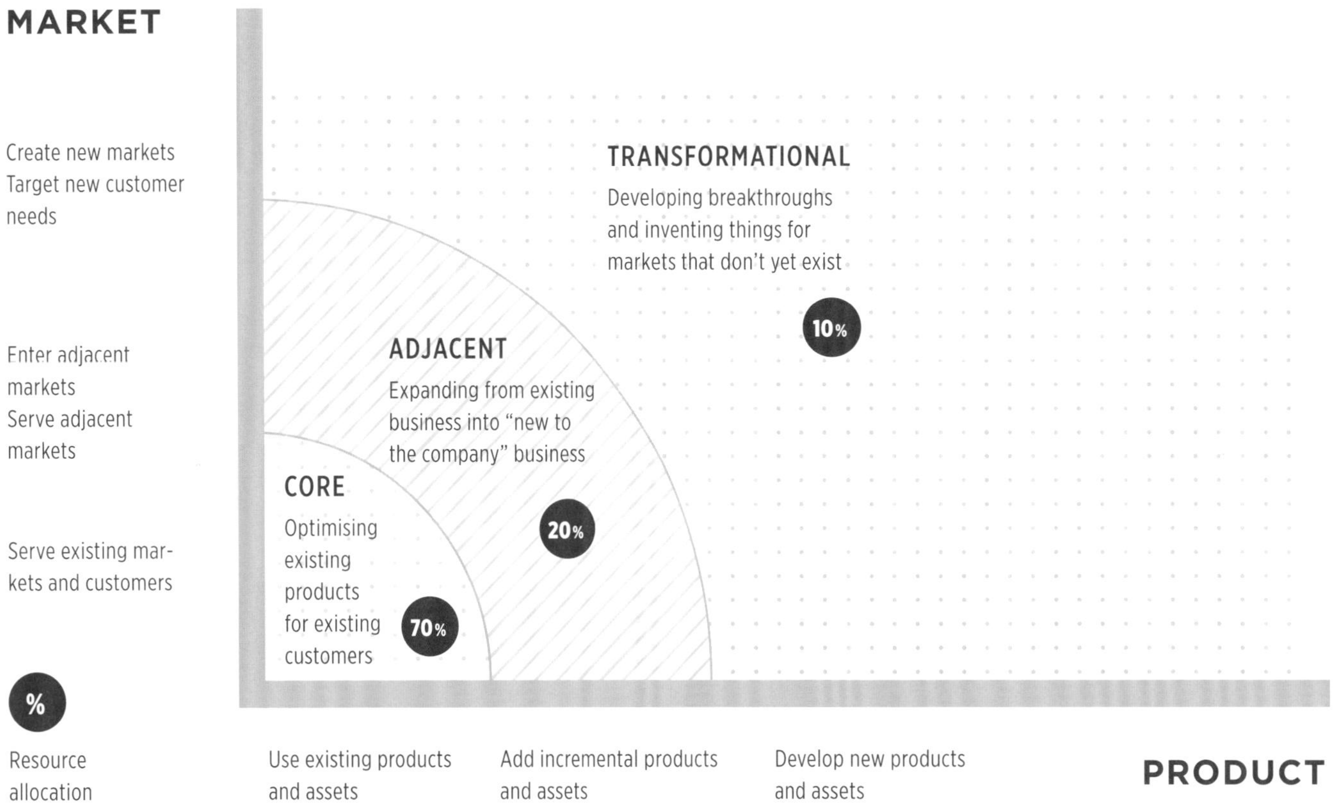

MARKET

Create new markets
Target new customer
needs

TRANSFORMATIONAL

Developing breakthroughs
and inventing things for
markets that don't yet exist

10%

Enter adjacent
markets
Serve adjacent
markets

ADJACENT

Expanding from existing
business into "new to
the company" business

CORE

Serve existing mar-
kets and customers

Optimising
existing
products
for existing
customers

70%

20%

%

Resource
allocation

Use existing products
and assets

Add incremental products
and assets

Develop new products
and assets

PRODUCT

FIGURE 1 › THE INNOVATION AMBITION MATRIX
Source: Nagji and Tuff (2012).

their products outdated or, worse, obsolete. This is not a new phenomenon. As Vice President Hayden Hill of The Clayton Christensen Institute argues:

> *"It's what Netflix did to Blockbuster and what your digital camera did to your old film camera, but also what the Ford Model T did to the horse and buggy".*

These external forces shake the status quo of the existing businesses and change the rules of competition: *"It's not enough to keep pace with industry stalwarts"* [1].

The solution for almost all is seen as innovating – with "doing better" being the key to bringing new products and services to market with enhanced features and better services, or to leveraging products into adjacent markets bringing forward new revenue potential. This approach to innovations confirms the truism that *"most of the time, most innovation is incremental"* but what about new, breakthrough, novel or radical innovations? Again, the leading commentators suggest that this is a small proportion of the corporate portfolio, but conversely has the potential to offer the largest returns, if only it can be harnessed effectively.

As you can see in the figure above, sourced from the works of Nagji and Tuff [2], and entitled the Innovation Ambition Matrix (›see Figure 1 on the left), innovative firms typically focus on their core markets, offering incremental innovations that optimise and extend the life of their existing products and customers and that takes up 70% of their efforts.

But in the face of consumer behaviour shifts, technology development and growing market uncertainty, companies embraced a variety of initiatives to drive more far-reaching, new or novel innovations – which we refer to as *radical innovations*. We have witnessed these initiatives ranging from establishing a company presence in Silicon Valley (or other technology or trading hot zones), setting up internal venture capital funds, experimenting with open innovation partnerships, training employees in design thinking, creating lean start-ups and spin outs, adopting future thinking and foresight methods, – the list goes on. These are all examples of how companies have gone about establishing the enabling conditions within their organisation whilst gaining the skills for planning, launching and hopefully succeeding in delivering radical or breakthrough innovations – but for each of these successes, there are also

[1] **BUSINESS MODELS**
Moreno H. (2017). *Reinventing business models in a disruptive world thought leaders.*

[2] **INNOVATION PORTFOLIOS**
Nagji & Tuff (2012). 'Managing your innovation portfolio'. *Harvard Business Review*, 90(5).

far more examples of these new and novel innovations failing!

Just look at the recently opened Museum of Failure in Sweden. The museum curator Dr. Samuel West indicates that *"Innovation and progress require an acceptance of failure"*. It is commonly accepted that to succeed and reach to the top, you have to learn from past failures. Interestingly, a recent study published in NATURE[3] focusses on natural human behavioural mechanisms that govern our response to failures. The study suggests that there are only small differences in how people react to failure, but these can lead some into stagnation whilst others, it will stimulate the necessary conditions to move a subject beyond a tipping point and eventually lead to a success. I guess this reinforces the mantra *"if at first you don't succeed – try, try again!"*

3 UNDERSTANDING FAILURE

Yin, Y., Wang, Y., Evans, J. A., & Wang, D. (2019). 'Quantifying the dynamics of failure across science, startups and security'. *Nature*, 575(7781), 190–194.

One common misconception when comparing radical and incremental innovations is that the growth phase of the offerings will occur at the same stage. This is not the case and a study conducted by Arthur D. Little shows that companies expect the revenue contribution from breakthrough products launched over the last three years to double in the next five years from 8% to 15%.

INCREMENTAL INNOVATION

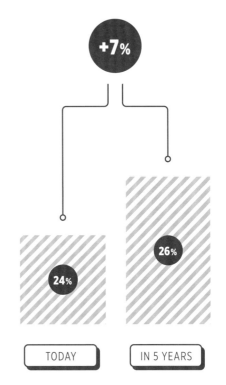

FIGURE 2

Incremental vs radical innovation growth expectations

BREAKTHROUGH INNOVATION

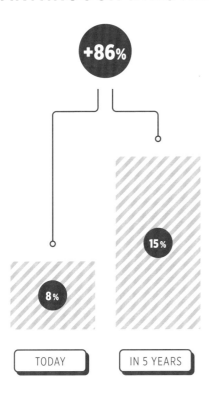

+86%

15%

8%

TODAY

IN 5 YEARS

Source: Arthur D. Little Breakthrough Innovation Survey, 2015.

The expected contribution from incremental innovation is expected to rise from 24% to 26% over the same period of time (›see Figure 2). This means breakthrough innovations have the ability to offer big returns, but might take a long time to get there, whilst incremental innovation leads to faster results but with way smaller returns.

The results of this and numerous other studies indicate that it is hard to deal with breakthroughs, but if you do the returns can be large. It also confirms that radical or breakthrough innovations require different capabilities, structures, approaches, success metrics and culture to succeed.

This is why many organisations shy away from radical innovations. In fact, when trying to bring change into an organisation, you don't have to go very far to hear the phrase *"that is just not what we are about"* or *"we don't do that around here"*. This rhetoric whilst underplayed in many board rooms, can be the cultural showstopper that kills off new and novel innovations, and has been likened by scholars to a *"corporate immune system"* that attacks good and bad ideas alike – killing them off due to their unknown nature.

CORPORATE IMMUNE SYSTEM

From the minute an organisation is born it starts to develop its own unique way of making sense of its environment, identifying and resisting threats – just like a human immune system. This helps keep the company on-track and focussed on what should make it successful. If it finds something new, novel or that it can't make sense of, its automatic response is to reject it.

To combat this internal immune response, one common trend seen in high-profile MNE organisations is to undertake their breakthroughs in isolation and often in secrecy – being left to mature outside of the influence of existing markets, hidden from existing technology trajectories or shielded from existing customers who might not be ready or equipped to adopt these radical offerings.

To achieve this isolation some companies create small, specialist, agile departments that reinforce the idea that breakthrough innovations can be seen as being "in spite of" rather than "in harmony with" business as usual such as skunkworks, breakthrough factories, moonshot accelerators, whilst others start subsidiary companies or spin-outs.

These trends have led to a tendency for many corporate organisations to ponder different structural configurations – to try to decide which is best for their new, high risk ideas. Many examples are out there, such as GOOGLE-X – the breakthrough innovation team at GOOGLE, AUDI'S QUATTRO GmbH that aims to bring forward more radical innovations for AUDI; skunkwork originated in LOCKHEED MARTIN and is now widely used by other organisations.

» Any company designed for success in the 20th century is doomed for failure in the 21st. «

ACCORDING TO DAVID ROSE

FIGURE 3

Possible structural configuration to deliver radical or breakthrough innovations. *

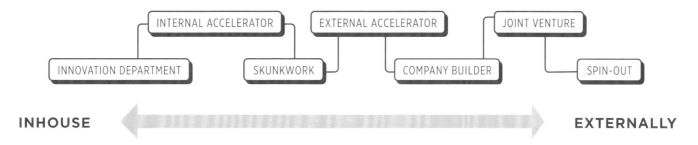

INTERNAL ACCELERATOR | EXTERNAL ACCELERATOR | JOINT VENTURE

INNOVATION DEPARTMENT | SKUNKWORK | COMPANY BUILDER | SPIN-OUT

INHOUSE ⟷ **EXTERNALLY**

* Comment: The authors acknowledge there are various organisational structures and also that various names are often used interchangeably.

What we have observed by studying organisations during our own research is that companies regardless of their size are not indifferent to these possible structural configurations as they are becoming more and more concerned about their future. As the serial entrepreneur David Rose [4] points outs *"Any company designed for success in the 20th century is doomed for failure in the 21st"* or alternatively predicts that, by 2028, *"40% of companies in the S&P index will be gone"*.

Our book therefore aims to offer insights, tools and techniques that illuminate the thought processes that shape decisions in terms of the organisational struc-

tures or forms that might work for your new, novel or breakthrough innovations.

Ranging from internal innovation departments to spin-outs (›see Figure 3), we recognise there is more than one way to structure your organisational efforts to pursue innovation.

The following sections of this book will explore your innovation ideas, considering their relative merits and explore some of the other unknowns before helping you decide which configuration might work for you. For example, is setting up and funding a *corporate innovation departments/labs* or *in-house innovation programme*

[4] **ACCORDING TO DAVID ROSE**

David S. Rose is an Inc. 500 CEO, serial entrepreneur, angel investor, author and keynote speaker who has founded or funded over 100 pioneering companies.

(often named an *internal accelerators* or *incubators* – owned and controlled by you; integrated within the organisation but often as a distinct department) better when it comes to your radical ideas?

Better than, perhaps, establishing a *skunkworks*, (existing geographically outside of your organisation, but funded and controlled by you, enjoying access to your key customers and having the autonomy to launch new products themselves), but then companies often enlist the help of *external accelerators* or *venture builders* (private independent companies, who train and hot-house cohorts of intra-preneurs to help them test ideas) to incubate or scale-up their ideas during a certain period of time.

    Again these structures in-turn are different from *company builders* (a private company that partners with you to set up a jointly-owned third-party company, sharing the costs and risks with you and providing expertise you lack in marketing or development) or *joint ventures* (legal entities, jointly-owned and managed with a partner or range of partners) or finally establishing an entirely new company, as a spin-out (wholly owned by you, but controlled by its directors and motivated by their fiduciary duty).

Skunkworks are great for creating a protected environments for your radical innovations, …

… but they do little to innovate the core business.

FIGURE 4

Key phases to structure
your innovation.

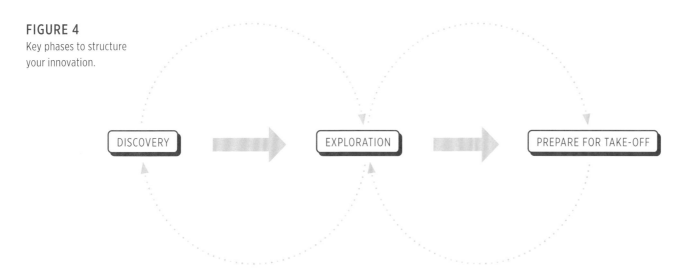

5 **CONWAY'S LAW**
Conway's law is an adage stating that organisations design systems that mirror their own communication structure. In other words: the way the company is structured – hierarchy, teams, divisions, etc. – might determine how the product will be sub-divided and worked on too.

It is named after computer programmer Melvin Conway, who introduced the idea in 1967.

Wow, who knew there were so many variations! 5 And to be honest these are only the variations that we could come to a consensus on – and we know that in different parts of the world these terms are often interchangeably, or sit across some of the structural differentiations we have noted, but please go with us on this.

Adopting a playbook style, organised in three key development phases (›see Figure 4) namely: *discovery, exploration* and *prepare for take-off*, we present key questions and considerations to help you develop and explore the potential of your ideas within the relevant structures. Our canvases are built within each phase and supplemented by case studies and examples that exhibit a variety of organisational structures that we hope will lead you to understand your innovation and make suggestions on how you might choose to structure your innovation team around the challenges you face.

We realise that you are not necessarily starting from scratch and might not need to go through all phases.

EXTENDING
EXISTING BUSINESS

Market with high potential but risk of
resistance from the established business.

COMPANY BUILDER
EXTERNAL ACCELERATOR

DISRUPTING EXISTING
BUSINESS

Dealing with new markets creation
by proposing new solutions.

SPIN-OUT
JOINT VENTURE

SUSTAINING EXISTING
BUSINESS

Manageable without organisational change.

INNOVATION DEPARTMENT
INTERNAL ACCELERATOR

DEVELOPING RADICALLY
NEW TECHNOLOGIES

High potential, necessity to build
new skills in an efficient way.

SKUNKWORKS

FIGURE 5
Which model? Towards a simple rule of thumb.

THE AMBITION OF INNOVATORS

A new theme of research and corporate coaching in this area, developed in the US by Nagji and Tuff, the idea that innovation can be focussed on core markets, adjacent or breakthrough markets, is becoming a pivotal decision for many marketing or innovation directors.

Therefore, in Chapter IV you will be able to consider your planned market and how your → PROPOSITION will begin to penetrate this market and gain sales. You will establish if your proposition is new to your organisation or a market you know well. Once you have established this, we then ask you to consider your corporate capability and skillset. Is this innovation something you can deliver with only minimal in-house development, or does it represent something that might be a real step change for your company?

By thinking about your proposition's maturity, you can begin to see (›using Figure 5 left) that there are immediately possible structural options that might help you. But it can't be that simple, can it?

Well, we think at this stage we are definitely on the right lines, but to be totally confident we need to dig a bit deeper, before we can be sure which structural model is right for you.

We believe this is what makes our playbook unique as we aim to offer key help and guidance in navigating this potentially painful set of decisions – to skunk or not to skunk? Is "in-house" best when it comes to new, novel and breakthrough innovations?

→ PROPOSITION

Proposition is a common term used in the entrepreneur's and innovator's discourse – meaning the new idea, the innovation project or the offering you wish to bring forwards.

PART 2

RECIPES FOR SUCCESS DURING YOUR INNOVATION JOURNEY

CHAP

DISCOVERY, EXPLORATION AND PREPARE FOR TAKE-OFF: PROCESSES AND ORGANISATIONAL STRUCTURES

Chapter III outlines the menu for processes and organisational structures... once you know what is on the table you will have the opportunity to explore your ideas or aspirations.

WITH ALL THE RESOURCES AND CAPABILITIES YOU NEED TO FLOURISH.

⇥ Definitions see next page

In Part 2 we will navigate you through our playbook in terms of the phases of your innovation journey. Moving from ⇥ DISCOVERY where your ideas might secure minimal investment, ⇥ EXPLORATION begins to flesh out the idea with potential development plans, before setting up the key resources and activities by ⇥ PREPARING FOR TAKE-OFF, so that eventually you can successfully bring your innovations ⇥ TO LAND.

One of the questions you might ask at this point – are any of these phases more important than others? In short, whilst we know this is an ever-debated topic, with creative-types focussing on idea development, entrepreneurs on resource acquisition and configuration and scaling and marketeers urging for market intelligence, we encourage you to take the innovator's view[1] – where in-depth planning and carefully controlled implementation in each of these stages will lead to projects with a greater likelihood of success (in most cases). OK, so not in every case – but by failing we learn far more[2], so every step we take in this process pays dividends even though at the time this might seem hard to reconcile.

So with a focus on our key phases of innovation (*discovery, exploration* and *prepare for take-off*), we have

[1] MANAGING INNOVATION

Tidd, J., & Bessant, J. R. (2018). *Managing innovation: integrating technological, market and organisational change.* John Wiley & Sons.

[2] FAILURE DRIVEN INNOVATION

Alexander, A., Berthod, O., Kunert, S., Salge, T. O., & Washington, A. L. (2015). *Failure-driven innovation.* Artop GmbH.

**3 FRAMING
PROBLEMS**
Bessant, J., Öberg, C.,
& Trifilova, A. (2014).
'Framing problems in
radical innovation'.
*Industrial Marketing
Management*, 43(8),
1284–1292.

established from our own research (and based on the research of others)[3] that various *formal organisational roles and structures* can directly contribute to configuring and enabling the development of innovations and that this is equally as important in each of these key phases.

DISCOVERY

When it comes to the discovery phase, it is common for companies to *conduct the discovery phase internally,* where traditionally R&D department had responsibilities for new or improved offerings. In the past 20 years however, a variety of approaches designed to generate ideas internally (from across the company) or externally (i.e. outside-in or inside-out practices for example corporate venture approach to partner with start-up ecosystems or involve employees in internal innovation challenges, hackathons, etc.) have been adopted – which in turn have led to different temporary or permanent organisational structures. For example, companies might have in-house innovation programmes responsible for generating ideas, where they encourage their staff using a range of motivational tools to submit

→ **DISCOVERY**

involves a variety of activities to create, identify and elaborate ideas and help to articulate emerging opportunities. In the discovery phase, firms are faced with high uncertainty and the goal is to identify any assumptions that can potentially lead to failure and help firms to quickly explore and abandon them; identify alternatives that might work in case the initial idea fails. This phase is sometimes identified as ideation or new ideas generation.

→ PREPARE FOR TAKE-OFF

involves securing resources and designing a roadmap to quickly move the proposition to the next level. In this phase, your goal is to shift from a successful experiment and start designing a fully operational business. At the end of this phase, the proposition will be assessed to establish if it is ready or not for landing.

→ EXPLORATION

involves finding evidence that ideas have business potential. Exploration involves identifying and testing the most critical assumptions of the proposed idea in order to build a promising business case. During this phase the goal is to confirm that there is a problem-solution fit and possibly a market-solution fit. This phase is sometimes referred to as incubation.

→ LANDING

is the key phase where the focus is on building a business and the necessary infrastructure, turning habits into routines to ensure business functioning (independently or within the company depending on the chosen organisational forms).

their ideas to online platforms. Likewise, the staff can rank the ideas, in terms of the idea's potential and thus group-select the most beneficial. Examples of this were the "IdeeClick" platform developed by Orange and France Telecom in the early 2000s; Innovation Jams by IBM or the Global Innovation Gig (GIG) by Volvo cars.

4 HIGH-INVOLVE-MENT INNOVATION

Bessant, J. R. (2003). *High-involvement innovation: Building and sustaining competitive advantage through continuous change.* Wiley.

Now the employee suggestion box is not a new idea[4] and extensive research has provided best practices in developing these platforms and for some firms they are highly successful but for others they come with a realisation that they often only create incremental ideas – a bit of "do better" innovation that directly rewards the staff inputting the idea. Often these approaches are agnostic to the nature of ideas generated and mostly result in building solutions that fit the existing business[5].

5 PRODUCTIVITY DILEMMA

Benner, M. J., & Tushman, M. L. (2003). *Exploitation, exploration, and process management: The productivity dilemma revisited.* Academy of management review, 28(2), 238–256.

Firms trying to reach further afield for their ideas can employ dedicated, specialist resources focussed on boundary-spanning and extended search activities. For example, STMicroelectronics in the semiconductor industry, Lundbeck in the pharmaceutical industry amongst others. They employed dedicated staff responsible for seeking out radically innovative ideas and they do this by forming alliances and partnerships. These

THE EMPLOYEE SUGGESTION BOX IS NOT A NEW IDEA... AND FOR SOME ORGANISATIONS THEY ARE INVALUABLE.

OPEN INNOVATION IS ABOUT LEVERAGING YOUR NETWORKS.

staff members (often holding positions as open innovation or external relations directors) have rich external networks and expertise in matching and extending some of these opportunities.

Similarly, some companies also engage independent "hunters"[6], whom they commission explicitly to seek out new, novel and radical innovations. Hunters are responsible for identifying both internal and external opportunities for innovation (the potential inside-out and outside-in functions of open innovation)[7] but set against the aim of identifying new-to-the-company or new-to-the-world innovations.

One way to deal with internal bias toward incremental ideas is to partially externalise the discovery phase by engaging in truly open innovation practices. This can be by seeking advice and ideas from partner organisations (such as universities and other R&D intensive organisations) who are becoming more conversant with how their research can influence new commercial development and are offering their intellectual property via internet-enabled platforms (such as Marblar); or by harnessing people-power, by creating open innovation platforms that crowd-source ideas from the

6 RADICAL INNOVATION

O'Connor, G. C., & DeMartino, R. (2006). 'Organizing for radical innovation: An exploratory study of the structural aspects of RI management systems in large established firms'. *Journal of Product Innovation Management*, 23(6), 475–497.

7 OPEN INNOVATION

Chesbrough, H., & Brunswicker, S. (2013). *Managing open innovation in large firms*. Garwood Center for Corporate Innovation at California University, Berkeley in US and Fraunhofer Society in Germany.

8 King, A., & Lakhani, K. R. (2013). 'Using open innovation to identify the best ideas'. *MIT Sloan Management Review*, 55(1), 41.

general public that can then be explored internally (such as Innocentive).[8] By creating campaigns that focus on particular challenges (similar to those seen on the Royal Shell Dutch – Game Changer platform) companies are able to seek out solutions from across the globe and then fund the exploration of these, before deciding if they wish to use them in their own innovation activities. It is important to note that during the discovery phase the organisers of these campaigns need to be careful not to discourage radical or breakthrough ideas and regimes to enable this must be included within the collection, ranking and decision processes.

Hopefully for the most promising ideas, the *discovery* phase then leads to *exploration*. It is through this phase that we will be able to accurately separate the ideas that are worth pursuing.

Stop! we hear you shout – everyone knows that this process is not linear. Hold that thought and let us complete our explanation of the phases first.

IDEAS FROM WHERE?

Independent of the structures within your company, there is an increasing recognition that innovative ideas can come from every corner of the organisation, both in and outside of its boundaries. The capacity of organisations to identify the idea's potential and then capture and nurture them is crucial for the future success of these firms.

BUT IT IS NOT LINEAR?!

We totally recognise that innovators can start directly in the exploration phase, or might start with exploration but then realise that some critical knowledge is missing bringing them back to the discovery phase – BUT we also know that it is essential to have a high-level process setting-out the key steps that need to be taken for the innovations to be successful. Therefore we will continue to present our book in a linear fashion but we will suggest you can dip in and out of each chapter (V, VI and VII) according to where you find yourself at any particular point of the innovation journey, regardless of if you think you are going forwards or back-tracking!

THE MAIN GOAL OF EXPLORATION IS TO EVIDENCE THE IDEAS' POTENTIAL OR TO KILL IT QUICK!

EXPLORATION

The exploration phase is key to understanding the potential of radical ideas: for the organisation internally; for its clients or customers and for its stakeholders. Therefore, in this phase the company will explore what it realistically takes to deliver the potential of the ideas and whether it makes sense for the company to invest further (with a view to at least completing the exploration phase).

The main goal of exploration is therefore to map out the potential of the idea or to kill it as fast as possible by providing evidence of what works and what does not. We all know that companies usually have many ideas, but it is extremely hard to spot the good ones. It is through careful experimentation and learning that you will be able to validate the potential of your idea. This phase therefore consists of creating and testing a number of working hypotheses from which to formulate some form of a minimal viable (or near working prototype[9], i.e. using lean start-up methodology proposed by Steve Blank initially and further developed by Eric Ries). Many companies use the form of design sprints to conduct the exploration phase in a timely manner.

9 MVP
Reis, E. (2011).
The lean startup.
New York: Crown
Business, 27.

10 DESIGN SPRINT
Knapp, J., Zeratsky, J., & Kowitz, B. (2016). *Sprint: How to solve big problems and test new ideas in just five days.* Simon and Schuster.

Design sprints[10], initially introduced by Google Ventures, help you to test and develop prototypes in a timely manner.

Now, one common mistake in this phase is to conduct tests solely with your existing clients.

For example, if you present them with an emerging opportunity and ask if they are willing to buy it in the future: they will most probably say yes if the idea is within their current business interests (even if they don't intend to buy one). Or, alternatively, they will just reject it, but the responses can be indiscriminate or just poorly informed. Henry Ford once asked North Americans what they would want in the form of an automobile – and they said they just want faster horses. Thus, in the exploration phase only concrete and reliable signals must be used as calls to action and carefully planned market engagement, undertaken to show evidence of consumer interest, is essential. Likewise, innovators need to be clear about what they are testing[11] and why. During this phase, experimentation skills for prototyping, technology development and market testing; business development and user-centric design are highly beneficial.

11 AGILE METHODS
Morris, L., Ma, M., & Wu, P. C. (2014). *Agile innovation: The revolutionary approach to accelerate success, inspire engagement and ignite creativity.* John Wiley & Sons.

ONE COMMON
MISTAKE IS
TO ONLY TEST
WITH YOUR
EXISTING CLIENTS.

START-UP STUDIOS

Start-up studios are company builders that aim to build several companies in succession. A variety of different models exist: *investor, incubator, builder and corporate excubators*. For example, investor type studios like GV, Science or The Family bring in early stage external start-ups or ideas and help them grow. They provide both funds and expertise. Incubator type studios like Founder, Spartas-tartups get equity in exchange for their inten-sive work with each team. At Founder, every year, 50 of the most innovative start-ups from universities are selected and each team is awarded up to $100K. After 12 months of ex-tensive work with each start-up, they invest in the most promising ones. While investor and incubator studios mostly invest in the existing (even early stage) start-ups, builder models like Idealabs, App'n'roll, Barefoot & Co and Wefound focus on creating companies from scratch based on ideas generated internally by the studio or proposed by other actors.

As a result of the many uncertainties in the exploration phase, increasing numbers of companies have now set up internal accelerators or incubators, internal innova-tion departments and innovation labs. Companies are also trying to build the skills required for exploration:[12] GE has embraced the "experimentation mindset" and has trained more than 60,000 employees in lean start-up methodology, while others set up inter-disciplinary teams to help successful intrapreneurs test their ideas. For example, Le Plateau of Société Générale was set up to help internal start-ups explore their potential.

Alternatively, companies can also turn to the expertise offered by external organisations to test the potential of their ideas (external accelerators or company builders). In general terms, incubators, innovation labs and accel-erators are mostly driven by market validation without necessarily conducting technical explorations. What we have discovered is that when the original creator of the idea moves to be within the external accelerator or START-UP STUDIO, this shift expands their points of reference and yields a greater vision as they learn how to use the agile processes and resources provided in these locations. This in turn creates a work culture orientated around a more flexible and faster start-up

[12] **LEAN FOR CORPORATES**

Whilst corporates understand the ne-cessity to continually innovate they strug-gle to keep inventing new solutions and business models. To enable this some create new organi-sational structures and build teams with complementary skills enabling the change from execution to exploration. Lean start-up models and minimum viable offerings are one popular way of fram-ing these shifts.

mindset than when the individual and the project are retained within the organisation. This is particularly useful when testing market uncertainties. Accordingly, when technical uncertainties are also high, the firm should decide carefully whether an external organisation is better positioned to explore the solution.

Often the incubation activity undertaken in in-house or external accelerators will only last three months, although in some cases this can be extended by an additional three months, if decision makers agree to invest further resources. During this time, it is crucial to document the process and internalise the learning carefully, thus building a body of evidence that substantiates why it is worth continuing into the next phase. In some cases, when the incubation team takes charge of an idea and conducts market tests, they can tend to generalise their findings and interpret the results in the wrong way – we pay careful attention to this risk, in our canvases provided in Chapter VI.

INCUBATION PERIOD

Interestingly enough, the idea of three months came from tourist visas' duration, which in the US are only three months. We are not sure if this is a reflection of tourists being used on a test basis for ideas and we perhaps suggest not – but perhaps it is the idea that if you can't see all that you need to see in a new location in three months, then you're not trying hard enough?

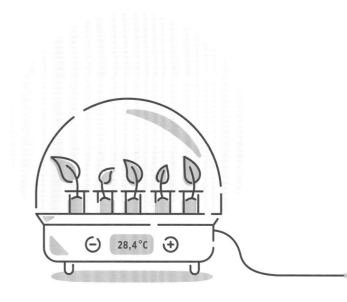

A LITTLE PROTECTION GOES A LONG WAY FOR THE MORE RADICAL IDEAS.

Likewise, other organisations prefer to create even greater degrees of separation between their originating company and the exploration teams – using models which we refer to as → SKUNKWORKS. In these circumstances the idea owner may or may not move into the skunkworks, working alongside a team of specialists who each represent different parts of the organisation (or are recruited as specialty designers, engineers, etc. similar to a model of start-up studios or company builders but are established from internal departments) to aid the project development.

The originator of the term skunkworks was the development team at Lockheed Martin called The Skunk Work, who brought America the first supersonic military aeroplane, to outperform the development work of their enemies and competitors in the early 1950s. Kelly Johnson and his team designed and built the XP-80 in only 143 days leading to the establishment of the first skunkworks. For more than 50 years, the team of scientists and engineers at Lockheed Martin show that it is possible by anticipating tomorrow's capability gaps and solving the most critical US national security challenges. Why name it The Skunk Works? The team were housed in a second-hand circus tent, located next to the site of a bad smelling plastics factory and the term was adopted from a popular cartoon of the time, which depicted a factory making "Skonk Oil" out of old skunks, shoes and other waste materials.

Skunkworks however are not cheap to set up and require systemic effort when providing resources and sustaining operations from the host departments. As an alternative, other organisations tend to undertake the exploration phases entirely independently of the originating firm – by setting up a new legal entity such as a spin-out, joint venture or other subsidiary. Here the exploration is undertaken and managed under the critical eye of the new directors and shareholders and where resources are introduced to the subsidiary in the form of structured loans, senior lending or by raising capital through the sale of equity. Exploration can then proceed relatively unhindered by any relationships with the originating company and freedom to explore that these models offer have shown to be very successful for certain companies and certain radical innovations. For others they have been entirely unsuccessful.

→ SKUNKWORKS

A skunkworks is a group within an organisation given a high degree of autonomy and unhampered by bureaucracy, with the task of working on advanced or secret projects.

PREPARE FOR TAKE-OFF

Here is when ideas, resources and individuals really come together as the project *prepares for take-off*. The activities in our Chapter VII deal mostly with assembling and deploying resources and addressing any further uncertainties:

IMPORTANCE OF PURPOSE

To succeed in implementing your innovation journey – you need to define your "meaningful direction" or purpose. This is important for all phases of innovation, but crucial in "prepare for take off". Having a clear direction will make the selection of your next steps so much easier.

▷ Who has to be on board?
▷ How to protect the idea?
▷ How to scale it?
▷ How to bring it to the market?
▷ Which resources are required at the start?
▷ Which routines need to put in place?

Again, in this phase, it is crucial to decide whether the idea should be connected with the originating company; developed externally with company builders; or even sold on to other interested parties. Thus, the evidence generated in the exploration phase is critical to making an informed decision; however, this phase is often neglected and we routinely see companies rush on to launch projects trying to get the results as fast as possible. Alternatively, this phase is where projects get killed off because we did not identify the right customer

THIS PHASE IS OFTEN NEGLECTED AND WE ROUTINELY SEE COMPANIES RUSH ON TO LAUNCH PROJECTS KEEN TO GET THE RESULTS AS FAST AS POSSIBLE.

base or stakeholder community within which to launch the innovation. Many "techno-push" ideas are killed in this phase. For example, in 1990 the CEO of Intel, Andy Grove was convinced that their video conferencing idea, ProShare, would be a huge market. After five years and $750 million in investment, they realised that the perfectly working solution was just not in demand – the environmental conditions turned out not to be present. So, don't rush to land here and take the preparation for take-off as your opportunity to avoid Intel's mistake – mistakes that 25 years later Skype and more recently Zoom have not repeated; the major environmental shift being pandemic isolation and mass, global social distancing creating the Zoom-Boom of 2020.

Another reason we have identified for an internal idea to be killed off in the preparing for launch phase is that the novel character of the ideas can often appear "life threatening" for other internal business units (i.e. originally when the company set out to exploit its cash cows, and these drove the company revenue up accordingly, it is unlikely that succession planning took place that considered how these units might end). If these business units are influential, even though they may have a rapidly shrinking market share, they can still

fend off the new radical innovations. For this reason, we pay particular attention to collecting and analysing the most evidence-based forms of data in the canvases (›presented in Chapter VII), such that carefully argued decisions can prevail. However what we have noted from our research is that hiding these radical innovations is still a very popular way of keeping them secret to both staff, competitors and customers and so perhaps this phase is where most people will assume that organisations are most likely to select a vehicle outside of their normal operations.

Communicating widely across and outside the organisation at this stage can help secure resources; identify the right partners and prepare for the future of the project; whether it will be conducted with an external accelerator, company builder or internally within an existing or brand-new organisational structure. Business accelerators often source ideas internally or partner with external start-ups to help them test and scale faster. For example, ST-Up was set up by STMicroelectronics (the largest European chipmaker). ST-Up is their 18-months-long acceleration program entirely dedicated to providing access, technical knowledge and expertise, tools, resources and connections to hard-

EXIT STRATEGY
In a start-up or spin-out it is recognised that there is likely to be an exit strategy – for originators, for investors, etc. so they move on to new things – but this exit strategy is rarely in place inside a company and thus staff in these departments assume they will go on forever, if they continue to hunt for efficiency savings).

ware start-ups from Israel. ST did not take any equity from the external start-ups but asked them to sign non-recurring engineering agreements. Another example, Wefound, backed initially by Engie, is a corporate start-up studio that partners with big corporations to create start-ups using shared resources and a multidisciplinary team.

Finally, in Chapter VIII, *readiness for landing*, our final canvases help teams to reflect if they are ready to move on to launch or if they need to consider further work across *discovery, exploration* and *prepare for take-off*. Again, the company should decide whether the solution should be further developed internally, or if a partnership or other vehicle is required.

The readiness for landing can be considered regardless of where the projects have been undertaken in house or using one or other of the various structural models we have begun to highlight above. At this stage, you might find that the company's most suitable landing plan can exist outside of the organisation. *Spin-outs*[13] allow employees to form businesses outside of the main organisation often with the initial team recruited from within the company. Universities and research institutions use this strategy extensively. For example, a research institute, CEA Leti in France, has established more than 60 successful spin-outs in 50 years. From this cohort, Soitec – specialized in generating and manufacturing high performance semiconductor material – was created in 1992 and now has more than 1,000 employees. IKSN, launched in 2014, developed a tablet that digitalises handwritten drawings, notes and sketches in real time. They managed to raise $2 million in October 2014 to commercialise the product. Alternatively, *joint ventures* allow companies to partner with other established organisations and develop ideas collaboratively. This is particularly useful when complementary skills are needed to develop breakthrough ideas, combining together the relative strengths of each organisation and often lowering costs of production and thus minimising risks. One great example is the billion-dollar video service Hulu, which came about through the collaboration of Disney-ABC TV Group (The Walt Disney Company), Fox Broadcasting Company (21st Century Fox) and NBC Universal TV Group (Comcast).

We encourage our reader to consider each and every stage of the process as largely independent as they make their plans, and to consider therefore each stage

13 SPIN-OUTS
CEA Leti (2019). *Deep tech for edge artificial intelligence,* press kit.

EACH STAGE CAN USE DIFFERENT STRUCTURES – IT IS ABOUT ALIGNING YOUR INNOVATION CHALLENGES WITH THE RIGHT STRUCTURE.

as having a potentially different structural configuration as the projects or portfolio of projects dictate. A summary of these stages and the respective canvases used to assess the ideas and develop the innovations is shown in Figure 6 below.

OK, we promised to go back to this issue of linearity – we now hope you can see that our process follows a logic in terms of progression, but there is absolutely no reason you cannot hop around from canvas to canvas and section to section, as your ideas develop, move forward, identify a hurdle, overcome, move forwards, take a setback, revisit the market analysis, etc.

Thus the process described in this book is iterative and we recognise that it will take different pathways for you or your team as you develop the skills and competences to undertake these tasks, but we hope our book provides a useful structure to guide your learning and also we hope our canvases provide rigor and reliability that will aid you in this process.

We acknowledge we are not exhaustive and realising the potential of your ideas depends on many factors (i.e. novelty; skills at hand; market maturity; detailed

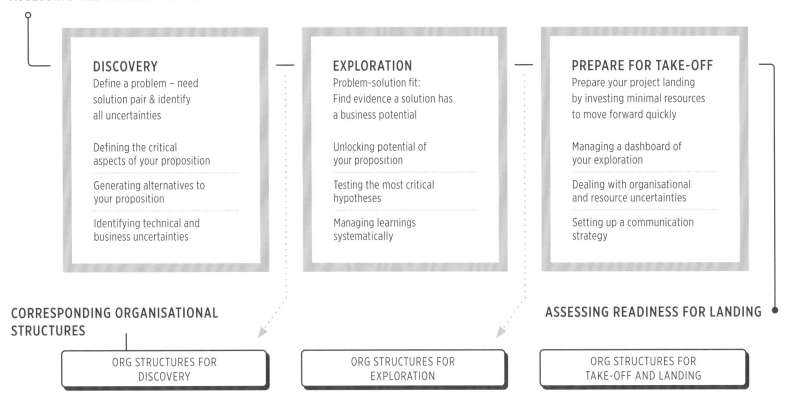

ASSESSING THE MATURITY OF YOUR PROPOSITION

DISCOVERY

Define a problem – need
solution pair & identify
all uncertainties

Defining the critical
aspects of your proposition

Generating alternatives to
your proposition

Identifying technical and
business uncertainties

EXPLORATION

Problem-solution fit:
Find evidence a solution has
a business potential

Unlocking potential of
your proposition

Testing the most critical
hypotheses

Managing learnings
systematically

PREPARE FOR TAKE-OFF

Prepare your project landing
by investing minimal resources
to move forward quickly

Managing a dashboard of
your exploration

Dealing with organisational
and resource uncertainties

Setting up a communication
strategy

CORRESPONDING ORGANISATIONAL STRUCTURES

ASSESSING READINESS FOR LANDING

ORG STRUCTURES FOR
DISCOVERY

ORG STRUCTURES FOR
EXPLORATION

ORG STRUCTURES FOR
TAKE-OFF AND LANDING

FIGURE 6

Schematic of the radical innovation canvases in discovery, exploration and prepare for take-off.

WHAT YOU HAVE LEARNED

▷ You need a different philosophy for each phase

▷ Phases can be linear but mostly you hop back and forth in our process

▷ Structures can be designed to support the development of your ideas

▷ What worked last time might not work this time – be open to different structures if your ideas call for it

knowledge of the sector itself, etc.), but we hope our book provides enough knowledge and guidance to help you with radically new ideas. We also believe that carefully following our canvases is even more crucial for managers who, perhaps rather than focussing on one project at a time, are managing an *innovation pipeline*[14]. A portfolio approach (where core ideas, adjacent and radical ones are part of the portfolio) needs to establish greater rigor and order, due to different ideas being at different maturity levels. A portfolio approach will allow organisations to balance risks and ensure positive outcomes for their innovative portfolio by using various structural models to create an agile, configurable and flexible range of options for each and every project. This is because when you pursue radical innovation opportunities, there is one thing we know for sure: they do not happen overnight.

14 INNOVATION PORTFOLIO

For more reading on innovation portfolios, please check a book from Alexander Ostelwalder and colleagues, *The invincible company.*

Osterwalder, A., Pigneur, Y., Smith, A., & Etiemble, F. (2020). *The invincible company: How to constantly reinvent your organization with inspiration from the world's best business models.* John Wiley & Sons.

CHAP

ASSESSING THE MATURITY OF YOUR PROPOSITIONS

Chapter IV will help you to identify where your proposition stands in terms of maturity and whether it has to be managed as an early stage innovation project. This is definitely a must read if you don't know where to start.

FROM LITTLE ACORNS MIGHTY OAKS GROW – BUT NOT ALL OF THEM.

I f you have an idea you want to explore; you are managing a team with multiple ideas or you need to assess the innovative potential of ideas within your organisation, how do you decide which ideas should have a "green light"? This is normally the starting point for most organisations and thus this is where the more practical part of our book really commences.

Or perhaps, as a manager, you receive many ideas every day: How do you decide which ones to move forward and how will you do this? How do you structure your innovation portfolio? How do you adjust your organisational structure to support these ideas? How do you allocate precious resources? Well, firstly, we need to assess the relative maturity of ideas in your portfolio.

It is important to first identify if you are dealing with high uncertainties and also what is the relative maturity of your proposition? To assess the maturity of your proposition and suggest relevant phases, you will need to think about *different types of uncertainty: business, technical, resource and organisational uncertainty*[1]. When facing high uncertainty you need to learn about market drivers, value for your customers and any parties within the value chain and make sure that your

[1] **MORE ON UNCERTAINTY**
Arteaga, R., & Hyland, J. (2013). *Pivot: How top entrepreneurs adapt and change course to find ultimate success.* John Wiley & Sons.

business is viable *(business uncertainty)*; you need to understand whether the proposed idea is feasible technically *(technical uncertainty)* and you are clear that it is the best solution to address customer problems (problem-solution fit). Furthermore, you need to be aware of *resource uncertainty*, in particular, how you are going to secure resources, people and competencies from within or from outside of your organisation. Finally, is your organisation fully on board? Who will support the development of your solution? *(organisational uncertainty)*. For more detailed definitions of different types of uncertainty and ways to manage them, please refer to Chapters V and VII where you will deal with these uncertainties in detail.

At this stage, you need to be aware of the uncertainties you face to determine the right navigation sequence of canvases to get you to launch as quickly as possible.

So, are you ready to start?

First, you need to identify where your proposition stands in terms of maturity and whether it has to be managed as an early stage innovation project (›see Canvas 1):

NAVIGATING THROUGH UNCERTAINTY

Make sure you keep your chin up. These early stages can seem daunting as essentially this is where we take you on a journey to establish what it is you know and inevitably it will bring to your attention what you don't!

○ *Does your proposition deal with an established market?*

○ *Is the value clear for your potential customers?*

○ *Are these potential customers ready or willing to pay for this solution?*

○ *Or is your value proposition need-to-have, important for your customers (or only nice-to-have)?*

○ *Do you have skills and competencies to develop your proposition internally?*

○ *Did you secure resources to develop your proposition? And finally, is your organisation onboard?*

WHAT VALUE, FOR WHOM?

What is crucial here is to be aware of the fact that tools and methods that you will use to deal with your innovative proposition highly depend on the level of maturity of your idea. For instance, if you are still unsure of what your solution is, it does not make sense to calculate its economic viability. Instead, you need to focus on what is the potential value of your future solution and for whom. You need to verify if there is any particular pain point to address. Once you have a clear notion of what your solution will look like and the value it brings to the market, you will be able to define the total addressable market, total accessible market, develop your business plan, secure funding, find supporting stakeholders. Your first steps are highly dependent on the level of uncertainty that you are dealing with and the radicalness of your proposition. Therefore, when approaching your idea maturity, you need to consider technology, market, resources and organisational uncertainties.

These questions are not exhaustive, but they will help you to realise where you stand.

If you can answer all these questions accurately and you are sure you have validated your technical and market uncertainties; you are clear on the value that you propose to your potential customers (and internally for your company) and you are confident you can launch quickly – and most importantly you have robust evidence to support these claims, then probably no need to read on – our book is not designed for you!

If it is not the case, you might be still dealing with high uncertainty or the potential of your proposition needs to be explored, then it is time to commence with ⊸ ASSESSING THE MATURITY OF YOUR PROPOSITION. Based on the quick assessment below, you will be aware of challenges that you face and indications on the relevant phases and canvases for you to work on.

CANVAS 1.1 › **HOW MATURE IS YOUR PROPOSITION**
Please answer the following questions to determine where your proposition stands.

PROPOSITION DIAGNOSIS

	NO I DON'T KNOW **0**	YES I AM CERTAIN **1**
Does your proposition deal with an established market for your company?		
Is the value clear for your potential customers?		
Are they (customers) ready or willing to pay for your proposition?		
Is your value proposition need-to-have, important for your customers?		
Do you have skills and competencies to develop this proposition internally?		
Did you secure resources to develop your proposition?		
Is your organisation onboard to support the exploration phase?		

TOTAL SCORE

Please add up all
your scores.

CANVAS 1.2 › **ANALYSING YOUR SCORE**

Please consider your score and use the analysis below to guide you through the relevant steps.

3 – 5

EXPLORATION

You could start in the exploration phase. Are you dealing with an existing or a new market for your organisation? Do you have expertise required to develop your idea internally or do you require new competences? Are you sure of your market-solution fit before quantifying your market?

We suggest you can start with Chapter VI, but if your struggle come back to Chapter V.

0 – 3

DISCOVERY

You should start in the discovery phase. It appears you might not be entirely sure about your customers, their pain points or how promising your proposition could be for your organization – you are not 100 % clear on your idea – this section is perfect for you. In other words, your problem-solution fit is not there yet.

You should start with the proposition description worksheet and Chapter V.

5 – 7

PREPARE FOR TAKE-OFF

Congratulations, you seem to be on a good track. Perhaps you should still check if your solution is ready. Go to Chapter VII. If you find you are struggling to answer the questions then perhaps come back to the earlier chapters.

CANVAS 1.3 › **SELECTING APPROPRIATE STRUCTURES**

Use to help you identify your main challenges & identify which structures could help you. Please select one quadrant by considering the target market and your expertise level.

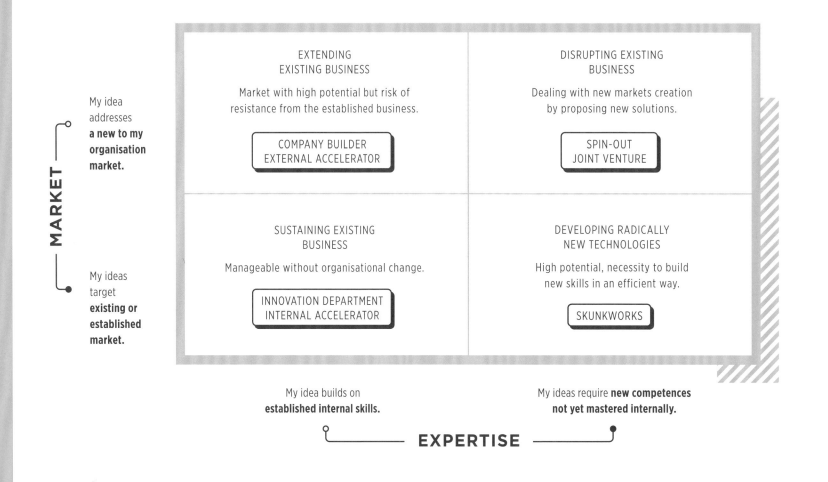

MARKET

My idea addresses **a new to my organisation market.**

My ideas target **existing or established market.**

EXTENDING
EXISTING BUSINESS

Market with high potential but risk of resistance from the established business.

COMPANY BUILDER
EXTERNAL ACCELERATOR

DISRUPTING EXISTING
BUSINESS

Dealing with new markets creation by proposing new solutions.

SPIN-OUT
JOINT VENTURE

SUSTAINING EXISTING
BUSINESS

Manageable without organisational change.

INNOVATION DEPARTMENT
INTERNAL ACCELERATOR

DEVELOPING RADICALLY
NEW TECHNOLOGIES

High potential, necessity to build new skills in an efficient way.

SKUNKWORKS

My idea builds on
established internal skills.

My ideas require **new competences
not yet mastered internally.**

EXPERTISE

So you can see – the pathway to your innovation can take a number of routes – if you have scored your ideas now you can move on to Chapter V, Chapter VI or Chapter VII – but remember if you jump a phase (because you are confident in this aspect of your idea – you can always come back if it becomes clear you need more confirmation to be sure).

CHECKLIST

- ☑ No need to rush to prepare for take-off and landing that require more traditional product development skills.

- ☑ Check carefully if your proposition is subject to high uncertainty and has to be managed as an early stage innovation project.

- ☑ Think of different types or uncertainty that your proposition might face (including technical, business, organisation and resource).

- ☑ Imagine how these uncertainties can affect the potential success of your project.

- ☑ We suggest you don't skip challenges just because you have not addressed them properly – keep at it and slowly reduce your unknowns.

HEY WE REALISE THIS CAN BE TOUGH! BUT DON'T SKIP CHALLENGES JUST BECAUSE YOU HAVE NOT ADDRESSED THEM PROPERLY – KEEP GOING!

Different organisational structures can be available within your company to support internal innovative initiatives (›see Canvas 1.3). You can conduct a quick check of common organisational structures based on the type of market you are trying to develop and expertise you would need to use to develop your idea. We will discuss these structures in detail in Chapters V, VI and VII.

Illustration – assessing ideas maturity in the banking industry

A large European semi-cooperative bank with multiple branches across Europe, active in both retail and private banking, as well as holding a significant stake in publicly traded investment, established an innovation lab to focus on the discovery and exploration of ideas.

The innovation lab's first step was to collect ideas from different branches and units within the company to seek out the potential of new ideas for different bank branches and their corporate operations. Any employee could suggest an idea for consideration. Essentially the bank harvested four types of ideas:

BUILDING YOUR IDEAS PORTFOLIO

Different types of ideas are subject to different constraints and uncertainties. The exploration phase will help to test and further realise the potential of your ideas, particularly their potential as well as their type and relative maturity.

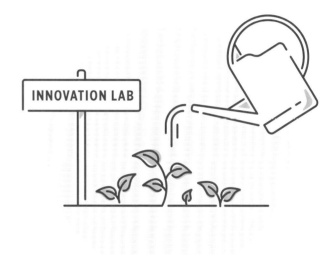

Grow your ideas
from different parts of the business.

CUSTOMER "NEEDS-DRIVEN" IDEAS

Ideas arising in the local branches were mostly related to the needs of clients. These ideas were directly driven by the market needs. Yet, the ideas were still not detailed enough or presented in an explicit enough manner to warrant direct investment in the solution; the product-market fit was not properly conducted; there were possible alternative solutions.

Example: *Replace the welcome desk with a digital assistant to welcome customers to the bank and direct them to the correct service channel.*

1

INTERNAL IDEAS

Ideas of different types arising from different bank departments or local branches. These ideas did not have direct customers calling for the service externally or sponsors internally who were prepared to invest in them yet. So, the lab had to "own" these ideas to explore their potential.

Example: *Using SMS to send and retrieve money to/from your bank accounts.*

2

TREND-BASED IDEAS

Ideas related to novel trends within banking or other novel areas; topics to explore that were considered as having potential long term.

Example: *Potential of AI for banking in general; blockchain to secure transactions and ensure transparency.*

3

CUSTOMER "NEEDS-DRIVEN" BUT MORE EXPLORATORY IDEAS

In this case, the ideas were clearly expressed by business units or bank branches but needed considerable evaluation, development and incubation because of the high levels of both business and technical uncertainties.

Example: *Secure, mobile bank mounted on a truck for access to remote areas.*

4

Examples of different types of ideas.

EXAMPLE OF CANVAS 1.1 › **HOW MATURE IS YOUR PROPOSITION**

Please answer the following questions to determine where your proposition stands.

MOBILE BANKING VEHICLE

	NO I DON'T KNOW 0	YES I AM CERTAIN 1
Does your proposition deal with an established market for your company?	0	
Is the value clear for your potential customers?	0	
Are they (customers) ready or willing to pay for your ideas?	0	
Is your value proposition need-to-have, important for your customers?		1
Do you have skills and competencies to develop this proposition internally?	0	
Did you secure resources to develop your proposition?	0	
Is your organisation onboard to support the exploration?	0	

TOTAL SCORE   **1**

Please add up all
your scores.

For each type of idea, the bank organised different discovery, exploration and prepare for take-off phases. When ideas were proposed at the lab, the idea maturity assessment was conducted by the innovation lab with the campaign managers and the decisions to place them into the discovery, exploration or prepare for take-off phases made accordingly.

The example on the left has been provided to illustrate how the *idea maturity* canvas can be used to assess the maturity of an idea received within the customer-needs theme by the bank (idea type 4, on p.60).

Idea: A mobile bank as a trailer or modular unit – that can be mounted/dismounted in 20 minutes to ensure on-spot banking services delivered in the temporary locations (i.e. concerts or festivals) or remote zones (i.e. mountain resorts or rural settlements).

Based on the assessment, the recommendation is to start with a discovery phase. It is important here to remember that uncertainties are context specific. The mobile vehicle might be novel for one organisation and something obvious for another one.

By conducting the organisational structure check (›see Canvas 1.3), this idea is dealing with a new to the bank market area using some of the available expertise – it is potentially *extending current business*. The suggestion would therefore be to use an external accelerator (or a company builder) to help explore the idea. In our example the bank decided not to use an external accelerator, but to create its *own internal accelerator in the form of an internal "innovation lab"*[2]. Even if the lab was essentially still part of the main organisation, it was set up as a separated activity, outside of business as usual and therefore was given the capacity to explore various solutions, operational configurations and assess the relative strength of the markets for each – some mainstream but some more novel. «

2 MORE ON CORPORATE ACCELERATION

Kohler, T. (2016). 'Corporate accelerators: Building bridges between corporations and startups'. *Business Horizons,* 59(3), 347–357.

CHAP

DISCOVERY: DESIGNING RADICAL IDEAS

Outlining all facets of your proposition, revealing underlying uncertainties and thinking of alternatives will help you to explore the potential of your ideas and articulate emerging opportunities. In addition, you will reflect on how ideation processes are supported within your organisation.

ASSEMBLING THE MOST
IMPORTANT DIMENSIONS
OF YOUR IDEA.

A *discovery* involves a variety of activities to create, identify and elaborate ideas and help to articulate emerging opportunities. When it comes to radically novel ideas, the discovery phase is crucial to help explore the full potential of the ideas. It is during the discovery phase that you can define the ambition of your idea: establishing how radical do you want it to be. Setting the scale of ambition here might help you to shift from incremental ideas to more strategic, radical or breakthrough ideas.

Defining the critical aspects of your proposition

OK – so you think that you have an interesting idea in mind and you are committed to giving the idea a try, but you still worry that your idea is not fleshed out enough to begin assembling resources and commencing exploration – so here is where you should start.

When dealing with new propositions – the sheer number of questions you might ask of your idea are many, and they all seem to come along at once:

- *What customer problem or potential business issue does your proposition solve?*

- *What is your target market?*

- *Are customers willing to pay?*

- *What are the inherent technical aspects and principles you need to determine for your solution?*

BUSINESS MODEL

A business model is simply a statement of your value proposition, how you will create it and also how you will deliver it and to whom.

We all know that successful innovations are the ones where technical solutions meet a particular need and thus offer value to the customers, but we also know that before we can do this there are many things that need to be considered – so before we even think about what our financial model might look like – first we must make the dimensions of our innovation explicit. Considering all aspects of your proposition here will allow you to define the exploration perimeter and make sure that you are not missing anything relevant at this stage.

Often we forget to think of all the solution aspects (i.e., we are too focussed on technology instead of being focussed on market outcomes or we are too focussed on markets and customers without thinking first if we can deliver the solution and if our solution would be the best one for the identified problem). We need to know the fundamentals of our ideas. Elon Musk uses the analogy of a tree: "Make sure you understand the fundamental principles, i.e. the trunk and big branches, before you get into the leaves/details or there is nothing for them to hang on to".

One thing we have learned from many, many corporate workshops is that an iterative approach to identifying and articulating ideas is hugely useful. Thus, before we signpost you to the work of Osterwalder and colleagues on value proposition design (also particularly relevant for the exploration phase), first let's think of a few fundamentals.

» Make sure you understand the fundamental principles, i.e. the trunk and big branches, before you get into the leaves/details or there is nothing for them to hang on to. «

ELON MUSK

When you are dealing with your proposition you need to think about:

- *What explicit value you are planning to deliver;*

- *To whom;*

- *Which customer problems you are trying to solve and what customer needs are you satisfying.*

These will help you shape the potential *value of your proposition.*

Let's unpack these with a few examples:

Thinking of value propositions and more importantly value to who? When Clarks shoes were developing their new customer loyalty programme in the late 1990s and early 2000s they stumbled on something quite new to them. They realised that there was not one, not two but three value propositions involved in the sale of their children's shoes!

Proposition 1 was simple – the child wanted a comfortable buying experience, in a shop that was quick to serve them and no scary measurement instruments or grumpy staff. They also wanted a shoe that lit up their imagination – made them feel special. A dinosaur emblem on the sole, an LED light array as they walked, glitter that didn't fall off; the list is endless, but this was only one aspect of the value proposition.

1

Proposition 2 was a little more complex. The parent wanted a similarly comfortable buying experience and a happy child, but they also wanted the right size, good quality materials, reasonably long-lasting build quality and a brand guarantee they could trust.

2

But Proposition 3, this is where Clarks stumbled on something innovative – the grandparent buying experience. So instead of just tailoring their experience entirely to the parents (and the child) they began to actively build value for the grandparents – a picture of them in the shop, showing off their grandchild and their new shoes – quickly dispatched to parents' phones, who in turn, were only too keen to realise the benefits of grandparent purchased new shoes! A great day out, some babysitting with a purpose, grandparent bragging rights and some new shoes to boot!

3

THINK ABOUT WHAT MAKES YOUR PROPOSITION UNIQUE, WHY DEVELOPMENT IS IMPORTANT AND WHY YOU BELIEVE IN IT – BUT TRY TO FOCUS ONLY ON WHAT MATTERS AT THIS STAGE.

Moving back to our proposition description – you now need to think of potential *usage scenarios*. We would encourage you to imagine at least two types of users:

○ *How and when do you think your solution will be used?*

○ *By whom?*

○ *How will the users interact with your proposition? What are the main steps?*

Furthermore, you need to consider relevant business models:

○ *How the value will be delivered?*

○ *Which business models are you planning to implement to introduce your solution?*

There are many resources available out there to help you think of different types of business models.

A very simple but powerful approach is the buy/pay/use framework.

USE OF BUSINESS MODEL CANVAS
You can make use of business model canvases as well, but we consider it more useful during the exploration phase.

In the example noted above – the child is the user (as is the parent), the buyer is the parent (with some influence from the child) but the novelty here is the grandparent moves into the role of the payer! (That's true even if they only top up the original budget and thus select Clarks over their competitors.)

ON BUSINESS PLANS

A common assumptions is that, in order to innovate, it is important to plan in fine detail: to know what things you need to do and to ensure management to have clear accountability and to manage their expectations. Reality rarely conforms to the plan once you start working and no business plan ever survives first contact with customers. So planning should be fit for purpose and flexible to change.

The initial description of the solution helps you to probe your first problem – cover things such as problem- solution fit; to identify missing elements and define your initial exploration perimeter (›see *proposition description* canvas below). This work will help you identify uncertainties related to your proposition. During the discovery phase your goal is to experiment, to play around and to start to gather evidence, but we are not there yet!

In a number of projects we have developed over the years there has been a distinct hesitance from the senior managers and company executives to accept any novel projects, even at this very early stage of discovery, that are unable to present detailed, numerical analysis of the markets, the development costs, the investment requirements and in some cases the likely costs and price point of the new products or services. We understand these things are important – but for our approach (and

EMBRACING UNCERTAINTY

At this stage some of the questions will be hard or even impossible to answer (in particular, if your solution is extremely radical). This is fine. The goal here is for you to realise things that you do not know at this stage. It is crucially important to be honest with yourself and it is totally acceptable to have uncertainty – just not in the launch phase.

for that matter any stage gate or open innovation process) to work there has to be an acceptance that in place of detailed numbers, indicative words and ranking is all that you have available at this time. No, this does not mean that these things will not come along – but you have to appreciate that the earlier in the process, the more you will be basing your decisions to continue on estimates and assumptions, most of which are not quantitative.

Illustration: WaterCo – exploring overall potential of your innovation portfolio during the discovery phase.

As an illustration – In 2010 WaterCo were market leaders in a particular suite of products for the water industry. They had a portfolio of eight products that, over a period of 30 years, proved themselves second-to-none in terms of performance and longevity. The problem however was the company was under pressure to increase their product range and capitalise on their highly technical design and manufacturing capability – the target – double digit growth! At first glance they had constructed (or at least bought-in) an innovation process system similar to a stage-gate system – but on closer inspection it became evident that they had brought forward only one or two product variations per investment cycle, even though they had more than 700 ideas saved up. These ideas had never been investigated. The problem was effectively a complex set of management checks and balances had been overlaid at the very start of the process that were so detailed, only the most incremental ideas were ever progressed. The company had become hesitant to do anything they couldn't provide detailed financial and market analysis for at the earliest part of the ideas stage. The solution was to implement a set of far less numerical and far more indicative questions, similar to the *proposition description* canvas below, that helped them make decisions and take actions to move forward with a wider range of ideas. The crux for the company was when the senior managers realised that by giving the green light to a project idea, in the discovery phase, they were only committing to move to the next set of checks and balances (and not to commit to launching the project at this stage)!

Indeed, in this phase the goal is often to find all the reasons the project might fail and learn from them in order to demonstrate what needs to be done to succeed.

ORGANISATIONAL DESIGN FOR INNOVATION

As a CIO or innovation manager, you need to see innovation as a flexible process – from start to launch. Your innovations need to be connected with the companies future strategic priorities but you as the innovator need to focus on building the right structural model to support your innovations. This creates tension between independence and alignment.

1 DISRUPTIVE INNOVATION STAGES

O'Reilly, C., & Binns, A. J. (2019). 'The three stages of disruptive innovation: Idea generation, incubation, and scaling'. *California Management Review*, 61(3), 49–71.

2 ABSORPTIVE CAPACITY

In contexts with high novelty, distant knowledge firms need to acquire their absorptive capacity

Kokshagina, O., Le Masson, P., & Bories, F. (2017). 'Fast-connecting search practices: On the role of open innovation intermediary to accelerate the absorptive capacity'. *Technological Forecasting and Social Change*, 120, 232–239.

So, you can see many of these elements will start to evolve once you start working on your solution and this is OK – and our canvases can be done again and again as details of the ideas begin to crystallise. Now to be clear we are not suggesting you should take shortcuts or avoid exploring all aspects of your proposition at this stage – just don't take a lack of information or an inability to detail costs right from the start as a signal to stop.

Don't forget you can question whether your idea has the potential to significantly grow the existing business, has the potential to renew it or even create a new one – this will please your senior managers, particularly if they are responsible for innovations that arise further into the future.

Things you might also consider:

○ *Try to spot what is novel about your idea for your organisation or outside. Does it really fill the ambition you initially set up? Is it worth pursuing? For example, at Amazon[1], new ideas are taken into consideration only if they offer different customer experience, have a potential to grown into a large business and provide great returns on invested capital in the future.*

○ *Consider if your proposition is about a new technology, new market, new value stream, new business models, new customer experience or new processes.*

○ *As an innovation manager in charge of the portfolio of innovations in your organisation, what are the best structures to discover the potential of the ideas in your portfolio? For example, is it high risk, high return; or more low risk, low return?*

Remember we define novelty[2] in terms of how the idea might be regarded within your company's existing activity, not just the market. Is the idea new to the world, or is it just new to you?

Imagine if Bosch, who is always near the top in terms of the worldwide market leaders for medium to high quality domestic appliances, brought forward the idea of having *an ultrasound cleaner*, similar to those found in the medical industry. This would be a novel step for Bosch. Even if the technology existed in the world, the products were specialist and high cost medical devices, not adapted for domestic appliances. Thus, the skills and technology were not necessarily in the existing business portfolio of the company, but the potential benefits were interesting to explore – high quality, fast and high-reliability cleaning with extensive water savings, reduced detergent use and thus reduced wastewater. This idea appears to be new, and thus radical for a company like Bosch, as well as for the domestic cleaning markets generally.

OK, so hopefully that is enough background, now you can start!

Below you will find the canvas that raises key questions to help you design and crystallise the first holistic version of your proposition and the empty one for you to work on your proposition. But here are some tips and checks for you to use as you go.

DEFINING YOUR PROPOSITION

Try to be explicit in defining all aspects of your proposition including value, usage, business model and technological principles even if they appear immature at this stage.

Once you have thought about all aspects of your proposition, determine if it makes sense and if so what is missing.

For each aspect, ask yourself how your proposition challenges the normal way of doing things within your organisation.

CHECKLIST CANVAS 2

☑ You need to have at least one element for each aspect of your proposition.

....

☑ At this stage, try to talk to a few recognised internal or external expert to collect their feedback.

CANVAS 2.1 › PROPOSITION DESCRIPTION

Please fill the canvas by focussing on the most critical aspects of your proposition.

VALUE & USAGE

USAGE SCENARIOS

BUSINESS MODEL DESCRIPTION

TECHNICAL DESCRIPTION

CANVAS 2.2 › **PROPOSITION DESCRIPTION**

Please use the guiding questions below to help you work on your proposition.

VALUE & USAGE

Who are your targeted customers
and target users?

What customer problem or potential
business issue does your proposition solves
(for each targeted customer group)?

Which customer or user needs are
you satisfying?

What added value do you deliver to your
customers and users? And other stakeholders
in the value chain?

USAGE SCENARIOS

How will your solution be used?

By whom?

How will the users interact
with your proposition?

What are the main steps?

Example: Airbnb booking (simplified)

1. User A logs into Airbnb.com with credentials.

2. User A enters destination, dates
and checks available property.

3. User A selects property
and contacts the owner.

4. After the request to book was confirmed,
the user books property.

5. User pays online using credit,
debit card, PayPal, etc.

6. User receives confirmation once
the payment is processed.

BUSINESS MODEL DESCRIPTION

How will the value be delivered?

Will you sell your solution?

Will it be rented or given for free?

At what price?

Which channels do you plan to use?

TECHNICAL DESCRIPTION

How will it work?

What is the underlying physical principle
or technological principle?

What is the role of each component?

How do they interact? How is the architecture/
integration envisaged? What equipment
and infrastructure are required?

Example: Imagine you work for one of the major automotive car manufacturers – BigCarCo.

BigCarCo's stated goal is

> *"to provide our customers with models that feature a delegated autonomous driving mode from 2020 onward. This technology will make driving safer and more pleasant while also freeing up time for drivers".*
> CHIEF ENGINEER, AUTONOMOUS VEHICLES

In broad terms, the race to create truly autonomous driving is becoming more and more competitive.

Many forecast reports are available for the autonomous industry: by 2040, three major automotive themes are set to emerge:

▷ the transition to electric,
▷ fully autonomous vehicles,
▷ and a higher percentage of people relying on ride sharing services as their primary source of transportation.

The report also indicates that approximately 98,000 fully autonomous vehicles will enter the market in 2020.

As one of BigCarCo's employees, you agree that an autonomous vehicle can be used to help the average person by taking over almost 100 % of their driving duties, replacing them with artificial intelligence, provided by a complex, proprietary in-vehicle computer system linked to a navigation and traffic management system, enabled by zero-latency 5G connectivity.

However, you must also keep in mind that many drivers will not wish to exchange their current vehicle. This is particularly true for both lower income drivers and owners of classic cars. You also note that many enjoy the driving experience and thus don't want autonomous controls enabled all the time. Your idea is therefore a partially autonomous computer system that can be retrofit to existing vehicles and that offers different degrees of autonomous control, depending on vehicle suitability, driver choice and road type – a type of partial autonomy.

You want to explore this idea further and based on the idea maturity assessment test (Chapter IV) you have realised that your idea needs further description – you are therefore still in the discovery phase.

First of all, you will need to further clarify your idea. Use the *proposition description* canvas above to begin to describe all the facets of your proposition and thus spot the unknown elements.

There is nothing more daunting than a blank sheet of paper – except possibly a host of unorganised notes and idea pages. You can start with a simple description of your idea:

Once you come up with the description of the first view of your proposition, it will help you to account for the missing elements.

VALUE: WHO IS IT FOR?

For current drivers, vehicle owners:

▷ enable the driver to be less attentive during commuting

▷ possibly opening up phone, work or safe social media time?

▷ ensure that they can commute on a traditional road – not a specially designed route.

1

USAGE: HOW IS IT USED?

▷ Used by existing car owners, who wish to move from one place to another, but who do not wish to buy a specialised autonomous vehicle.

▷ Drivers who wish to be able to talk, sightsee or potentially take control.

2

REVENUE MODEL

The vehicle can be rented; sold as an individual product and there might be a fitting service available for BigCarCo.

3

TECHNOLOGY

Sensors, partially embedded computer, head-ups display with advance warning systems, insurance with an integrated solution for the pre-existing vehicle, etc.

4

Generating alternatives to your proposition

Are you worried that your initial assumptions might be wrong? Have you just received a veto from your boss or investment team based on your current innovative proposition? This section is made for you – you can think of other options with the *alternative* canvas on page 81.

As you are dealing with early-stage innovation characterised by high uncertainties, the proposition you have in mind now might not be the best one in the future! To help you anticipate this situation, you will find here tips and tools to generate numerous alternatives to the initial solution you have in mind.

To generate alternatives, it is best for you to start by describing the first set of value and usage, business model and technical statements (›see *proposition* canvas on page 72) and then add in entire or partial alternatives that begin to explore each characteristic of your current idea – presenting possible alternatives as you go.

As the *proposition description* canvases help you think about your potential problem-solution fit, the *alterna-*

3 DESIGN THINKING
Brown, T. (2009). *Change by design: How design thinking creates new alternatives for business and society.* Collins Business.

PIVOTING IS PART OF AN ENTREPRENEUR'S TOOLKIT AND THE IDEAS WILL COME FROM IDENTIFYING PERTINENT ALTERNATIVES!

tives canvas helps you think of alternative scenarios for your ideas. By identifying the design of a potential product or service that fits with a specific time, or a set of specific criteria for the opportunities, you address what scholars call the "fuzzy front-end" of innovation. Think of alternatives that will help you not just iterate on your solution but uncover other categories to explore and even imagine new potential fields.

Alternatives can be seen as spaces for potential opportunity. They can help shape future scenarios and allow you to gradually choose the most suitable ones through experimentation. Alternatives can also be used to identify possible roll out and possible progression options – taking an initial idea and identifying how the second, third or fourth iteration might follow on.

Other tools and methods such as *Design Thinking*[3] or coming from other design theories like *Concept-Knowledge Theory*[4] or *Foresight and Future Thinking*[5] tools can help you work around these solutions!

This also begins to enlighten you to the potential of a pivot. Many of the world's most famous innovations started out their life as an idea for something else.

Example: Did you know that YouTube started out life as a dating site named USP that matched potential partners? The novelty in the innovation was the simple portal that enabled people to upload and share short videos of themselves. What USP had over other dating sites was short videos that told you far more about a person than looking solely at pictures ever could.

What happened was that users quickly discovered that uploading something funny was a good way to get views and thus get dates. Meanwhile the owners realised the upload portal's potential for more than just matchmaking – so they pivoted, showcasing video material alongside embedded advertisements and the YouTube phenomenon was born.

By working on your alternatives, you can take a step back and perhaps identify the predominant clichés of the particular market segment you are focussing on.

For example, consider:

▷ How does everyone else do it (in that field)?
▷ How do they make decisions?

4 C-K THEORY

Hatchuel, A., Le Masson, P., Weil, B., Agogué, M., Kazakçi, A., & Hooge, S. (2016). 'Multiple forms of applications and impacts of a design theory: 10 years of industrial applications of CK theory'. *Impact of Design Research on Industrial Practice*, 189–208.

5 FORESIGHT AND FUTURE THINKING

Gordon, A. V., Ramic, M., Rohrbeck, R., & Spaniol, M. J. (2020). '50 Years of corporate and organisational foresight: Looking back and going forward'. *Technological Forecasting and Social Change*, 154, 119966.

And therefore, what if you do just the opposite? How can you invert your proposition?

For example, you work in the soft-drink industry and you plan to design a new soda. You could think of something inexpensive, that tasted good and sweet and perhaps advertise it as an aspirational product, endorsed by a celebrity spokesperson. But is that the right approach for everyone? This is exactly what Coca-Cola, Pepsi, etc. have done.

Now think of an entirely different yet successful soda – Red Bull. It is more expensive than other sodas, has many strong ingredients and many think it tastes terrible – but it is also advertised as a product that can boost your performance in extreme sports competitions and has, as a consequence, gone mainstream as a means of pepping-up your day. This is an example of an *inversion*[6], which is a great way to generate alternatives.

Another alternative approach is to use the idea of *denial*[6]: What if you abandon completely the clichés that you have previously identified?

Again, as an example, think of when you want to open a bank account. You might imagine going to a bank building, close to your home or office, waiting for your turn in the queue, filling out the paperwork, proving your identity and providing your signature, witnessed by the clerk. You then receive your bank card several days later.

But what if you don't visit a bank, and see your bank agent, thus there is no waiting time, no paperwork and having a physical card is optional? This is exactly the model offered by Starling Bank, a challenger in the business banking network in the UK. Everything is done using smart phone technology – including uploading images of your face to prove your identity and recording spoken sentences on uploaded video that serve as your declarations (your name, age, address, etc.) and taking snapshots of your proof-of-identity documents. A couple of days of due diligence and background checks, undertaken by staff in the bank's offices using electronic records and online searches, and your account is available.

Or perhaps you could conceive of a solution that is out of proportion – *extreme scaling*[6]. For example, in the magazine industry subscription models still dominate. Magazines like VOGUE, MONOCLE or GENTLEMAN'S QUARTERLY (GQ) still charge upwards of 100 euros a year; or where alternatives offer heavy discounts on the

6 CREATING ALTERNATIVES
Several options are available to create alternatives. Among the most common are extreme scaling, inversion, denial. Consider as many as possible before settling on a single approach.

**CHECKLIST
CANVAS 3**

⊘ You need to have at least
one element for each aspect
of your proposition.

⊘ You have in mind at least 1
alternative proposition in case
your initial proposition fails.

⊘ You can now challenge your
initial and new propositions
by getting advice from a few
experts in your company.

annual subscription allowing you to pay around 50 %
less, in comparison with paying the walk-up price – say
20 euros a year for THE ECONOMIST for example. This is
possible due to scaling – so what if you pay only one
euro maximum for an online issue. You can use these
techniques to come up with your alternatives. Some
magazines like France's LE MONDE have explored similar offerings in the past.

So be ready to design your own alternatives using
the canvas below to guide you.

Going back to our illustration of the partial autonomous
vehicle control system:

1 — For the value and usage

One early development of autonomous vehicles is to
move goods exclusively. This is particularly good for
transporting raw materials around mining sites and
harvesting crops on farmland. Other options enable remote road repair using artificial intelligence and smart-
phones, such as RoadBotics. Now one way to look at this
development is to consider it an inevitable journey to
fully autonomous control, thus rendering the operator
redundant – but with a retrofit guidance system that

**ANTICIPATING THE
NEED TO PIVOT**

Generating alterna-
tives to your initial
proposition will help
you avoiding useless
loss of momentum on
your proposition if
you fail demonstrat-
ing your idea poten-
tial initially or the
proposition turns out
to be inappropriate.

You can propose as
many alternatives as
you can. Their feasi-
bility will be assessed
later on.

frees up the driver to carry out other tasks whilst still being in partial control of the vehicle, other productivity gains could be had. If you can free up some of the time for drivers, farmers and plant operators to carry out other, more sophisticated tasks, then who is to say that entirely autonomous control will pay off in these situations? Therefore, how do these things reflect on, alter the conditions for and change your thinking about the partial autonomous vehicle system?

2 — Alternative business model

As an alternative business model: could the systems be owned by IT companies or internet service providers (moving from B2C to B2B sales and support) and can be offered as free (through a data contract similar to mobile phones) or on a lease basis for the user?

3 — User behaviour

Another important thing to consider in all of this is *user behaviour.* Have you thought about the arrival of digital cameras and the role of photo-processing? The trajectory for this seemed obvious: with the advent of digital cameras, photo-processing stores quickly became few and far between and refocussed on high quality, professional markets only. The major technology companies quickly upgraded their home printer offerings – incorporating photo-quality paper handling and supplies, offering extended processing times to avoid smudging, developing stable and high luminescent inks and sophisticated ink-jets and nozzles. For a short period of time, some consumers bought these expensive printers, but the model for photos was changing ever more rapidly and with the advent of secure digital memory cards came the ability to eject your photos and thus have them printed for you. When the machines we now commonly see in supermarkets and other retail stores first appeared, quality photo printing again became something you paid for someone else to do and consequently the home printer market returned to competing on price, speed and basic features like copying and scanning instead.

CANVAS 3 › **GENERATE ALTERNATIVES TO YOUR PROPOSITION**

Add as many alternatives as you can.

TODAY	→	ALTERNATIVE 1	→	ALTERNATIVE 2
VALUE & USAGE What value do you deliver to your customers? Which of your customers' problems do you solve? How your solution will be used? What are the main steps?				
BUSINESS MODEL How will you sell your solution? Will it be rented or given for free? At what price? Which channels do you plan to use?				
TECHNOLOGY How does it work? What are the technical solutions? What is the role of each component? How do they interact? How is the architecture/ integration envisaged? What equipment and infrastructure are required?				

Identifying technical and business uncertainties and formulating hypotheses

As we have noted before, when dealing with radical or breakthrough ideas, we face extensive multiple uncertainties: technical, business, resource and organisational ones. During the discovery phase, we are almost entirely concerned with demonstrating the potential of the idea and then exploring technical and/or business uncertainties.

EMBRACING UNCERTAINTY

Again you need to be comfortable with uncertainty, later once you have identified the most critical ones, we have techniques to help you explore them in Chapter VI.

Once technical requirements are clear, specifications are relatively easy to compile and early prototypes can be developed, but at this early-stage, your project usually faces high levels of technical uncertainty: you don't even know if your solution is feasible, what the underlying technological principles are and how your chosen solution might work. When defining your technical uncertainties, you need to consider how comprehensive your scientific knowledge and expertise are. This will indicate if you should develop and deliver the idea in-house or in collaboration with other partners.

While dealing with more incremental innovations, your existing market or extended market offerings are likely

CONSIDERING THE TECHNICAL UNCERTAINTIES AND ALSO YOUR KNOWLEDGE AND EXPERTISE HELPS REINFORCE YOUR CONFIDENCE OR IDENTIFY YOUR NEED TO COLLABORATE.

more well understood and hopefully you understand your clients' business needs as well as their pain points. Likewise, you would normally have the data to support your business case.

But now your more radical proposition is facing higher ⊸ BUSINESS-RELATED UNCERTAINTIES: you don't know if your solution creates any value by resolving a particular customer pain or providing significant benefits, if your idea is economically viable nor if your target market is even willing to pay for it.

It is therefore crucial to identify as many uncertainties as you can that relate to your proposition and to begin to formulate → HYPOTHESES and construct challenging questions accordingly before moving much farther along.

Remember that at this stage, the way you see your future solution is your perception of *your version of reality* and thus needs to have a wider reality check. This version of reality, in terms of innovations, is what we refer to as the Innovation Paradigm. From the perspective of the firm it is how people view the firm and how employees and executives in the firm view themselves.

BUSINESS UNCERTAINTIES INCLUDE

▷ a degree of understanding customer needs and wants;

▷ the way the product or service will interact with the users;

▷ the degree to which you are clear about methods of sales and distribution;

▷ the potential in possible revenue models;

▷ and your market position in respect to competition.

→ **HYPOTHESIS**

A hypothesis or range of hypotheses are, in simple terms, assumptions that an idea proposed can be tested to see if it might be true or false.

REALITY LENSES

Each of us have a particular perspective or lens with which we view the world and the conditions within it. Extensive debate takes up arguments of nature vs. nurture (Dale Goldhaber – The Nature-Nurture Debates), thinking fast vs. thinking slow (Daniel Kahneman – Thinking Fast and Slow), various philosophies of knowledge (Polanyi, Kuhnian).

This is particularly relevant when we consider that the way an organisation is viewed and views itself can have enabling or destructive influence on new (to the company) breakthroughs and radical innovations.

For example, when Bausch and Lomb moved their business away from making sunglasses, renowned as the best in the world, to offering eyecare in the form of optometry, laser surgery, contact lenses, glasses and service-based provision on after-care products, the shift isn't all that surprising when considered from the perspective of the outside world.

The challenge therefore was to move their entire business from sunglasses to eyecare and to add in many service-based provisions to their existing retail operations. Had Walmart or Tesco (high street supermarkets) set out the same "vision" the response from the market might have been considerably different. Similarly, you might expect Volvo to shift into the partially autonomous cars market we discussed above. You might expect the same from Tesla, but what about from Nintendo?

Each of these names come with an immediate mental image and a set of mental constraints that determine

CHECKLIST

- List all the technical and business aspects that appear important to you! These aspects will constitute uncertainties of your proposition.

- Uncertainties need to be translated into hypotheses (assumptions that will turn out to be true or false) or open questions (to identify missing knowledge).

- You will not be able to deal with all hypotheses and questions, so you need to spot the most critical ones to address!

- To identify how critical each uncertainty is, check what happens if any of your hypotheses turn out to be wrong.

- Remember a hypothesis can be proven right or wrong, but a question will need an answer which in turn could be accurate or not.

how you think of them. Amplify this if you are an employee and you can begin to sense the power of the mental paradigm.

So now, list as many of the uncertainties related to your technical proposition, future users, clients, value that you bring, potential business model that you can think of (›see canvas below). If you have used the *proposition description* canvases, you might already have a good feel for the most important areas to deal with initially. This is a great ⊸ STARTING POINT.

At this stage, you might have assumptions based on observations (remember we call these *hypotheses*) or you might have more open *questions*. The goal is to formulate hypotheses that we can begin to test (to see if they turn out to be true or false).

Going back to BigCarCo, one of the assumptions could be that *"the company believed that people interested in partially-autonomous cars are willing to pay a $40 daily fee to rent one!" Or "we believe that AI is a technology mature enough to enable cars to completely control their passage safely through urban areas whilst drivers watch online media!"*

These are *hypotheses that can be tested.*

Questions, on the other hand, relate to missing knowledge. Questions are important when there is not enough knowledge available to define hypotheses and thus test them, or where there is a need to develop/access certain unknown components of your idea.

For example:

What will be the main activities of the drivers in autonomous cars? Will they still need to look at the road and, if so, how much of the time? I don't know how to integrate the AI technology into my current driving system. You won't be able to test these straightaway, but they are important questions that might require serious exploration (research projects) or create a need for you to identify experts to discuss your questions with.

Remember you will certainly not be able to test all the hypotheses or answer all questions, given the limited resources you most likely have access to (particularly at this early stage) but remember your goal is to demonstrate the potential of your ideas as fast as possible (or kill off the idea/promote a pivot).

ENTREPRENEURIAL MINDSET

We have led you toward the The Lean Startup by Eric Ries before, but this is an important philosophical perspective here – spend only what you need to decide if the idea has merit, or should be modified or killed-off – the philosophy therefore reinforces the entrepreneurial theory of fail, fail fast and move on!

Therefore, you would need to rank any assumptions you make first based on:

○ *What are the assumptions behind your idea that, if you found out they weren't true, would sink your idea?*

○ *What has to be true in order for you to succeed?*

Thus, you would need to prioritise your hypotheses and questions to spot the most critical ones that challenge the survival of the solution per se.

→ **HACKING MINDSET**

usually defined as believing "things are hack-able – that the way we've designed various systems is not pre-ordained or immutable. We can tinker, re-design, and play with them" Gorbis, M. (2013). 'The reality of what makes Silicon Valley tick'. *Harvard Business Review*, 9.

It's no surprise, therefore, that the most critical uncertainties should govern your allocation of effort and thus resources at this stage. Later you will need to design tests to reduce these uncertainties (confirming or overturning hypotheses or answering questions) as quickly as possible, with minimal effort and minimal budget (›see Chapter VI).

An approach to take is to develop a so-called → HACKING MINDSET here and use this opportunity to learn as much as possible to advance on your proposition. Be open to surprises and ready to adjust your plans!

CHECKLIST CANVAS 4

⊘ You have listed all the technical and business aspects of your solution that might be critical.

⊘ You checked (informally) if this list is complete with at least two technical experts, experienced engineers and experts from marketing, business development or a relevant business units.

⊘ Once all uncertainties have been listed, you have identified the most critical ones and built tests for each of them.

CANVAS 4.1 › **BUSINESS & TECHNICAL UNCERTAINTY**
Describe uncertainties related to your proposition.

WRITE YOUR FIVE* MOST CRITICAL BUSINESS
HYPOTHESES OR QUESTIONS

WRITE YOUR FIVE* MOST CRITICAL TECHNICAL
HYPOTHESES OR QUESTIONS

UNCERTAINTY ASSESSMENT
Assess the level of uncertainty of hypothesis
and questions related to your proposition.

* This number is indicative. You can have more than five hypotheses and
questions related to your uncertainties. Please aim to reveal the most critical ones.

0 No impact on
my proposition

1 I can easily adapt
my proposition

2 I need to seriously
modify my proposition

3 My whole proposition
collapses

CANVAS 4.2 › BUSINESS & TECHNICAL UNCERTAINTY

Please use the guiding questions and examples below to help you work on identifying uncertainties.

WRITE YOUR FIVE* MOST CRITICAL BUSINESS HYPOTHESES OR QUESTIONS

Think of a value-related hypothesis:
Which value does your proposition create for the end user?
To your client? Your company? A third party? Which problems will it solve?

Think of usage-related hypothesis:
How is it used? What are the main steps?

Think of business model-related hypothesis:
Who are you selling your solution to? How do you sell your solution? Is it economically viable? How will this solution be distributed? How will you organise the supply chain?

Autonomous car example:
Hypothesis: I believe that people interested in autonomous cars are willing to pay a $15 a day monthly fee to rent one.

Autonomous car example:
Question: What will be the main activities of drivers in the autonomous cars?

WRITE YOUR FIVE* MOST CRITICAL TECHNICAL HYPOTHESES OR QUESTIONS

Think of technology-related hypothesis:
What are the underlying technological principles of your proposition?
Are there any technical solutions already available on the market?
By whom? How does your proposition work?

Think of technology-related hypothesis:
What are the skills required to develop this proposition? Do we have the skills internally to develop this proposition? How you can industrialise your proposition?

Autonomous car example:
Hypothesis: I believe that AI is a technology mature enough to enable cars to completely control their trajectory.

Autonomous car example:
Question: I don't know how to integrate the AI technology into my current driving system.

UNCERTAINTY ASSESSMENT
Assess the level of uncertainty of hypothesis
and questions related to your proposition.

* This number is indicative. You can have more than five hypotheses and
  questions related to your uncertainties. Please aim to reveal the most critical ones.

[0] No impact on
my proposition

[1] I can easily adapt
my proposition

[2] I need to seriously
modify my proposition

[3] My whole proposition
collapses

ORGANISATIONAL STRUCTURES FOR DISCOVERY PHASES

When focussing on innovation, particular during early stages of the innovation processes, companies rely on different organisational structures to create supportive environments for their ideas to move on.

For example, when announcing new innovation strategies for a firm, business leaders might not even put together a structure (in particular for discovery) or identify a particular department to host the activity, deciding to make temporal arrangements instead. These are often called hackathons, start-up calls, agile business competitions, crowdsourcing or internal competitions and they focus on attracting people with a variety of backgrounds both internally and externally and motivating them to work collaboratively and to work quickly. Here, the goal is to access a variety of talents and skills that would not normally be asked to develop these solutions.

Our practice in running these has led us to realise that when this strategy is not backed up with clear exploration and resource appropriation phases, they gener-

ally fail to deliver on their early promises. Moreover, we note more success when organisations create activities that focus not just on motivating employees to be innovative, but also complement this with ways to help them to develop skills and competencies in innovation and thus develop new behaviours that can turn into habits. We refer to this as *developing an innovation culture within the firm* and we assert that it is hugely important, as we note in our introduction. Also, with using various initiatives to collect ideas during discovery, the firm looking for radical or breakthrough ideas should clearly set ambition for this to avoid ideas that are too obvious or incremental.

We do however note that the short-sprint *or* fast-iterative organisational forms can be used very effectively in the discovery phase – to start developing innovation processes within the company without implementing rigid structural forms at the start. This can help companies experiment in order to find the organisational structure that fits through trial and learning. This is exactly the situation with the *business innovation process* in the case depicted below.

TRIAL AND LEARNING

Loch, Christoph H., Arnoud DeMeyer, and Michael Pich. *Managing the unknown: A new approach to managing high uncertainty and risk in projects.* John Wiley & Sons, 2011.

Setting up temporary innovation lab in-house in the semiconductor industry

One of the leaders within the semiconductor industry decided to put together a temporary process to collect and explore ideas within the company in 2009. The lab was organised for three consecutive years with three campaigns: *Real Sense, Make Life Easier and Better* and *Green Energy*[7]. The main goal of these programs was to help develop solutions that could lead to multiple applications (and not leading to one particular market that the company was really good at) and even create new applications. During the discovery phase, submitted ideas were pre-selected based on their generic potential or even clustered together where the people who commented with ideas were brought together with different solvers and formed teams to build their initial propositions. Teams who were selected entered the discovery phase to formulate their business propositions, identify alternatives and create hypotheses to test in order to attract sponsors within and outside of the company. The temporary structure the company put together allowed for a rigid and clear process during the six months of the challenge. Each year the process was analysed and, based on the learning and feedback, new

improvements were implemented. The exploration process was conducted for winning ideas to help them test assumptions and develop first prototypes to be tested within the identified markets. This innovation activity resulted in several successfully commercialised products or even businesses that operate today (i.e. haptic technology solutions for the automotive industry).

Often the discovery phase is managed by internal innovation departments or *internal accelerators*. In November 2017, one of the largest of the world's banks launched a major internal *"intrapreneurship"* programme. The objective was *"to enable disruptive internal projects to emerge that will be the embryos of our future products and services, including projects that go beyond traditional banking services"*. Open to all staff internationally, the aim was to provide everyone with the means to become involved in the construction of new activities. More than 600 projects were submitted by staff and 144 projects were pitched to executives resulting in 70 ideas to be explored and tested. To avoid the usual mismatch between the ideas and the firm's priorities, an executive team consisting of 60 members participated in several workshops to identify priority areas and set up the ambition for the programme. The

7 INNOVATION CAMPAIGNS
Kokshagina, O., Gillier, T., Cogez, P., Le Masson, P., & Weil, B. (2017). 'Using innovation contests to promote the development of generic technologies'. *Technological Forecasting and Social Change*, 114, 152–164.

OFTEN DISCOVERY PHASE IS MANAGED BY INTERNAL ACCELERATORS... ALTHOUGH SOME CHOOSE EXTERNAL ALTERNATIVES.

company did not just organise a contest to collect some of the ideas, they implemented a process to explore and scale them. Thus, you must always think of the desired outcomes of the discovery phases and how you are going to manage them.

Some organisations use external entities such as *external accelerators* or *start-up studios* to help them think up new businesses. For example, Pathfinder was created as a branch of The Family (a start-up studio responsible for more than 250 start-ups) in 2016, to help corporates invent new businesses. Realising corporates struggled to deliver this internally they started by searching for problems to solve within the company's value chain and gradually design solutions and test propositions for them. Pathfinder argues that established players need to act more like fast-moving tech companies to become successful at innovation. By bringing in external entities at this stage, ideas can be explored outside of the company boundaries. However, our experience tells us that as a manager you need to be careful if you are planning to bring these ideas internally at some point: Who is going to own them? Who will develop them? How will you overcome the barriers within a "not invented here" syndrome[8] or use the advantages of the syndrome to your benefit?

[8] **NOT INVENTED HERE**
Antons, D., & Piller, F. T. (2015). 'Opening the black box of "not invented here": Attitudes, decision biases and behavioral consequences'. *Academy of Management Perspectives*, 29(2), 193–217.

«

CHAP

EXPLORATION: EXPLORING RADICAL IDEAS

Chapter VI should help prove that your idea is worth attention and that it has a promising business case. Exploring radical ideas can be tricky and we provide here tools and techniques to test the potential of your idea, manage learnings and unlock the potential of your offerings.

PLANT
RECOGNISER

EVIDENCING
THE POTENTIAL
IN YOUR
PROPOSITION:
SHOW NOT TELL.

A s detailed in the previous chapter, the discovery phase is where you establish your potential vision and try to make a case to move forward with your proposition. If you have followed the canvases provided you should now have a basic business proposal that can be defined as a set of hypotheses telling you what your proposition could enable in the market, which market and who will use the product, etc. In essence this is a very basic and sketchy business model together with a better understanding of what your solution is.

Exploration involves finding hard evidence and thus testing the most critical assumptions of the proposed idea in order to build a promising business case. The exploration phase is therefore not complete until your proposition (or set of propositions) have been tested. This will confirm "problem-solution" fit and potentially "product-market" fit. It will also help you understand what new learning you have gained and thus what needs to be done to take the next steps.

Unlocking the potential of your
proposition: identifying value sources

1 MANAGING
UNCERTAINTY

De Meyer, A., Loch,
C. H., & Pich, M. T.
(2002). 'Managing
project uncertainty:
From variation to
chaos (executive
briefings)'. *MIT Sloan
Management Review*,
43(2), 22–24.

Firstly, from our experience (and backed-up by empirical research[1]), dealing with highly uncertain projects and trying to apply standard investment metrics is almost impossible, or at least it is almost impossible to be accurate. We don't suggest you ignore the potential return on investments (ROI) or abandon the net present value (NPV) comparisons of alternative options – but perhaps leave these until later or at least realise they may be so inaccurate that they don't aid the decisions at this time.

Our rule-of-thumb here is the more radical the proposition, the less we know about the market (and the behaviour of the consumer) and thus the higher the risk (›see Figure 7). If you add in the idea that you might be trying to launch a systems-level solution, then we are entirely sure your accuracy in your detailed financial analysis may be limited.

DON'T IGNORE ROI AND NPV BUT ACKNOWLEDGE THEY MAY BE MISLEADING AT THIS STAGE AND THEREFORE NOT HELPFUL.

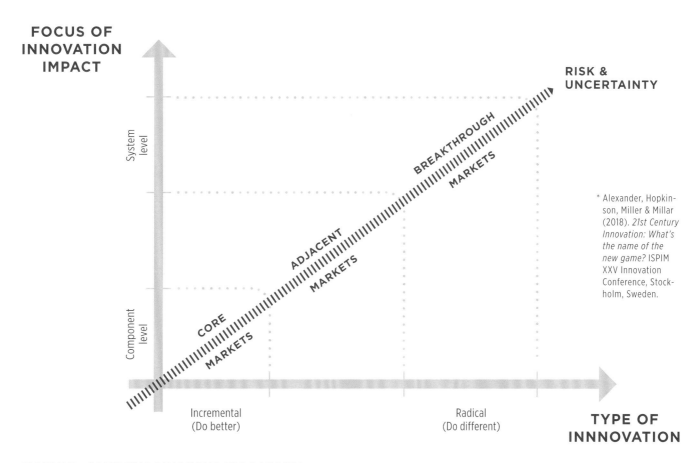

FOCUS OF INNOVATION IMPACT

RISK & UNCERTAINTY

System level

Component level

BREAKTHROUGH MARKETS

ADJACENT MARKETS

CORE MARKETS

* Alexander, Hopkinson, Miller & Millar (2018). *21st Century Innovation: What's the name of the new game?* ISPIM XXV Innovation Conference, Stockholm, Sweden.

Incremental (Do better)

Radical (Do different)

TYPE OF INNOVATION

FIGURE 7 › ASSESSING READINESS FOR LANDING

Innovation impact in regard to type of innovation (source: Alexander et al., 2018*).

Think about *Dragons' Den* (*Shark Tank* in the United States) and the point where the potential investors (the Sharks or the Dragons) are posing venture capital-style questions to the business owners, which amount to exercising a detailed business plan at the very early stages of their business. We all know intuitively, if the new proposition is radical and new to the world then the results are very likely to be wrong – but it still makes great viewing.

2 DECISION-MAKING

To improve decision making when dealing with new ideas intuition and reasoned and rational decision-making styles should be combined.

York, J. L., & Danes, J. E. (2014). 'Customer development, innovation, and decision-making biases in the lean startup'. *Journal of Small Business Strategy*, 24(2), 21–40.

The reality is that it is hard to estimate the total size of the potential market and combine this with your target clients' willingness to pay and *thus enable you to anticipate the future growth at the very beginning*[2]. *Yet, you still need to justify (internally and externally) why your proposition is worth pursuing*. This is especially critical when you are in the prepare for take-off phase.

Remember in the discovery phase, the go/no-go decision is often driven by intuition about the potential of the idea. To move out of the exploration phase, real evidence needs to be collected, and thus to onboard your sponsors and sell your idea internally, you will be expected to demonstrate the value or business potential of your proposition. We all know only too well that:

"an outstanding technical solution will not sell if it doesn't bring any real value to your potential customers"!

OK, so at this point we can tell you might want to be challenging this belief and reflecting on some of the most wacky inventions that oddly caught on, often for their novelty value alone – but how many of them are still being manufactured and sold now?

To understand the phenomenon of odd things catching on, we need to explore the characteristics of those doing the adoption. Everett Rogers (who we have referenced before) spent many years trying to categorise the criteria for adoption and also the characteristics of the adopters. He noted that many users are slow to take on new ideas and new products (particularly technical products), but he also identified a group of first movers, calling them "innovators" or "early adopters", noting they were "willing to take risks, are typically financially secure and had high levels of social status". These individuals often take the most radical innovations and they play with them – trying to identify and extract value and thus they can be important influencers and can set trends and determine fashions – but inevitably it is the long-term and slower-to-catch-on users that determine the value proposition that ultimately shifts the market to your products.

A fun example to recall is one of the world's first electric cars – the Sinclair C5. Invented by Sir Clive Sinclair in the 1980s, the small, single seater, three-wheeled, open top car had a small range, slow charging rate and was seen by many as being far too low to be safe from larger road users. Nevertheless, there was a short period where the early production runs sold-out, the product began to appear on average high streets and a national-level press "buzz" could be heard about the potential long-term market. In itself a great idea (as we all know the climactic and pollution related issues that electric cars might help to resolve) but the users community were all very much "innovators", according to Rogers' Theory. Thus, with an inability to win over the larger group of "early adopters" the popularity of the vehicle was entirely short-lived.

So, in the exploration phase you need to find a valuable market for your solution or put another way, you need to find the product-market fit. Start with the business problem you're trying to solve. Once validated, try to spot the stakeholders you are helping or bringing value

AN OUTSTANDING TECHNICAL SOLUTION WILL NOT SELL IF IT DOESN'T BRING ANY REAL VALUE TO YOUR POTENTIAL CUSTOMERS!

to. At this stage it is really important to make sure you have a sharp, accessible and clearly differentiating value proposition that brings outstanding benefits to your target audience.

3 VALUE PROPOSITION DESIGN

Osterwalder, A., Pigneur, Y., Bernarda, G., & Smith, A. (2014). *Value proposition design: How to create products and services customers want.* John Wiley & Sons.

Good tools to help you do this are the *business model* and *value propositions* [3] canvases developed by Strategyzer. By using these canvases, you should decide how your solution will be delivered (distribution channel, prescriptions, opponents, revenue streams). But if it feels like you are still surfing high uncertainty, you might need to come back to your business uncertainties.

Now, as we have noted earlier, sometimes the value to the business of your solution will be extremely hard to define (in particular, for radical innovation when the solution can lead to an entirely new market). If you find yourself here and the economic value is not obvious to define, you can enhance your arguments by identifying all potential value sources that your initiative might create for the company (often referred to as the socio-economic benefits) by highlighting the *non-financial elements that bring value to your project.*

BUSINESS MODEL CANVAS

We have not created our own version of a business model canvas. That seemed a little silly when we could just refer you to the work, which originated from the research of Alexander Osterwalder and Laurent Pigneur. It certainly has become popular and thus we don't think you can do much better than to use it. It is also available under a creative commons license – so what is not to like?

Stop – hold the line – Value? Hmmm, that is an overused and little understood word in the context of innovation!

Value is usually determined by the customers or the providers or through the mutual value offered.

Value can be defined as the assessment of the perception[4] of what consumers receive and give and values can be both intrinsic and extrinsic. Extrinsic value includes functional or utilitarian values and extrinsic social value such as interaction with a client. These are the values that we normally test for during our market tests. Intrinsic value includes the emotional, epistemic and intrinsic social value of a client.

When we speak of value, we do not limit this to the revenue potential nor to the relationship that the functionality of a thing has in respect to its cost to produce nor its retail price. Let's digress a little – your two authors are both surfers! Not very good ones by self-admission but nevertheless keen, and we can both talk in great depth about the relative quality in a set of waves and the value that surfing offers us. Not financial value, not performance versus specification or any typical business indicator or metric of value. But we and many thousands of others around the world value it nonetheless. The waves offer us many things – exercise and fitness, a space to think, a connection to the environment, education, a weekend pastime, a social scene to exist within, some form of identity and often something to talk about when we meet new people – the list goes on. We therefore urge you to think about the wider value proposition that your offering represents in terms perhaps of the social or the environmental value, whilst also narrowing it down to the income- and revenue-driven ones too.

Yet, here we take the concept of value and broaden it even further: we do not just consider the value for customers but for the company and its stakeholders as well.

4 **PERCEPTIONS OF VALUE**
Vargo, S. L., Lusch, R. F. (2008). 'From goods to service(s): Divergences and convergences of logics'. *Industrial Marketing Management*, 37, 254–259.

OUR WIDER CONSTRUCTS OF VALUE(S) CAN INCLUDE:

STRATEGIC VALUE OF THE PROPOSED SOLUTION

such as fit with your company's current or long-term strategy, potential to impact your company's position on the market, potential of your proposition in terms of competitive advantage in the future.

2

INDIRECT ECONOMIC VALUES

such as decreasing operations costs, helping on further promoting other products within the company and increasing their sales processes (i. e., by working on a complementary product) or even helping your organisation enter unchartered territories (i. e., see blue ocean methodology).

Blue ocean was proposed by W. Chan Kim from BCG and Renée Mauborgne from Insead with the idea that a market universe has red oceans that present all the industries today and the blue oceans – industries not in existence today. The methodology can be used to explore new value curves. For more details, please see here: Mauborgne, R., & Kim, W. C. (2005). 'Blue ocean strategy'. *Harvard Business Review*, 1, 256.

1

Think of how your idea can create value.

OPPORTUNITIES IN TERMS OF COMMUNICATION

such as opportunities to improve brand image, new strategic partnerships and overall, enhance your company's visibility.

3

OPPORTUNITIES IN TERMS OF DEVELOPING NEW COMPETENCIES

such as how competencies that will be acquired in this proposition can be used by other business units, new ways of working for the organisation or specifically the value of knowledge gathered in this proposition.

5

OPPORTUNITIES TO ENHANCE INNOVATION CULTURE

within the organisation, promote innovation and cohesion among the teams, hacking mindset and develop experimentation skills.

4

SOCIAL BENEFITS FOR DIFFERENT TARGET GROUP

such as policymakers, government, partners, providers.

6

5 **DISRUPTION THEORY**

For disruption theory, read HBR review by Bower, J. L., & Christensen, C. M. (1995). *Disruptive technologies: Catching the wave*

The main goal here is to define what is so great about your solution, why your company should pursue it and more importantly what the risks of not exploring this solution are? These might come from competitors developing the solution or from new entrants to the markets beginning to disrupt[5] your current business opportunities. Hence our *value identification* canvas is designed to help you reflect on the various potential sources of value and hopefully identify at least one action that you can deliver that will further enhance the value of your proposition.

THINKING ABOUT VALUE

Think why this opportunity is worth pursuing and what is the risk of maintaining the status quo for your organisation. Work on how to maximise the potential of your proposition across all categories: its strategic value, opportunity of enhancing communication, culture, developing new competencies and skills, creating indirect economic value.

CHECKLIST

⊘ You have answered the majority of the proposed questions.

⊘ You have identified at least three new actions to launch to improve the potential of your proposition.

CANVAS 5.1 › **VALUE IDENTIFICATION**

How many of these statements reflect your proposition? Think carefully what are the potential benefits of your proposition.

COMPETENCIES & SKILLS

Low Medium High
1 2 3

This idea will radically impact the positioning of my company in the market. ☐

The potential of my proposition in terms of competitive advantage is high. ☐

The proposition fits with my company's current and long-term strategy. ☐

PLEASE ADD UP ☐

›4 Great! No action needed!

‹4 Is it worth developing this idea internally? If yes, what can be done to improve its strategic value? Try to **identify at least one concrete action** to improve your score:

COMMUNICATION & NOTORIETY

Low Medium High
1 2 3

This idea will improve my company's brand image. ☐

This idea has a potential to establish new partnerships. ☐

This idea creates adhesion both internally and externally. ☐

PLEASE ADD UP ☐

›4 Great! No action needed!

‹4 What can be done to reinforce the notoriety of your proposition and strengthen its adhesion? Go back to the questions above and **identify at least one concrete action** to improve your score:

CANVAS 5.2 › VALUE IDENTIFICATION

How many of these statements reflect your proposition? Think carefully what are the potential benefits of your proposition.

Low Medium High
1 2 3

STRATEGIC VALUE OF YOUR PROPOSITION

This idea fosters the acquisition of
new expertise or new working methods. ☐

The potential value of
acquired knowledge is high. ☐

The proposition contributes to other
projects within the organisation. ☐

PLEASE ADD UP ☐

›4   **Great! No action needed!**

‹4   How can this proposition extend existing expertise within
your company? Go back to the questions above and **identify
at least one concrete action** to improve your score:

....

....

....

....

Low Medium High
1 2 3

INDIRECT ECONOMIC VALUE

This proposition can reduce
operational costs for my company. ☐

This idea results in sales increases
for our other products. ☐

This ideas could result in new market
creation for our company. ☐

PLEASE ADD UP ☐

›4   **Great! No action needed!**

‹4   Is there any possibility of creating benefits for other products, projects or processes? Go back to the questions above
and **identify at least one concrete action** to improve your
score:

....

....

....

Going back to our autonomous vehicle illustration: imagine as a BigCarGo employee, you want to promote the idea of developing autonomous vehicle control systems that will not be used on the busy roads, but only for executing the most difficult or time-consuming areas for driving, like parking, or for high-density areas, such as traffic congestion or roadworks.

The advantage is that you do not need to modify the entire vehicle's infrastructure but instead focus only on limited areas. When looking at the *potential value source* canvases, you can focus on:

○ *Competences and skills first: the potential of learning advantages and limits of using autonomous systems in difficult areas is huge for BigCarCo.*

○ *Developing expertise in managing the most difficult areas for driving might result in valuable learning for other departments that focus on both autonomous and non-autonomous vehicles.*

○ *This might present a great advantage for your company to enter a new "blue ocean" area.*

○ *Does it fit with your company's long-term strategy to have autonomous vehicles in place by 2030?*

As an action plan, you might consider developing a pitch deck or a communication booklet to clearly outline those benefits to potential sponsors within the organisation and organise meetings with them.

Testing the most critical hypotheses

As we mentioned the main goal of the exploration phase is to collect evidence that your proposition is feasible and addresses a problem that customers are willing to pay for.

To understand if there is a potential for a viable business, YOU NEED TO DESIGN AND CONDUCT TESTS to validate your proposition quickly, create the potential for a pivot or kill your proposition as early as possible.

These tests should be driven by the most critical assumptions. But remember, you need to be creative here and aim to spend as little resource as possible and conduct tests fast, to gain just enough information to make a decision. We would signpost you here to the work of Eric Reiss again – the idea being to create a minimum viable proposition (in the form of a proposal at this stage) and then test this with a potential customer base – noting what they value about your proposition and what they do not value. This enables you to alter and adjust your proposition as required. These tests will depend on the nature of your idea, its maturity and type of assumption (open questions or hypothesis). Please see Chapter V.

FOCUS ON CRITICAL ASSUMPTIONS FIRST

From our experience we would urge you to carefully consider the type of participants in your test group, as you are going to be relying on them to help you evaluate your MVP. Your group needs to have more than a smattering of early adopters and innovators or it is a hard sell and the results can often be unreliable.

Wrong assumptions can lead to wrong decisions: No matter how big your budget is, testing the most critical hypotheses should be on your task list.

Remember: each test should be driven by a particular hypothesis; you need to be clear with what exactly you are testing. Many innovators (and this is understandable) look for positive feedback of their ideas so they sometimes formulate questions that already set up the answer they want, by providing an answer as part of the question or they just talk to potential customers without having a clear hypothesis in mind.

NATURE OF YOUR TESTS

Be clear on what you are testing exactly and don't be seduced by false positive feedback.

VALUE IS SUBJECTIVE – LIKE BEAUTY IT CAN BE CONSIDERED TO BE IN THE EYE OF THE BEHOLDER. BUT TO MOVE FORWARD YOU HAVE TO ANTICIPATE POTENTIAL VALUES.

For each hypothesis, *you can use a variety of different tools* and sometimes they can be used in parallel or consequently (i.e. for example you could start with some semi-structured interviews with a set of target customers and then simultaneously you could create a simple web-based landing page that explains and details your product with an in-built sign-up option. This can then be posted across multiple sources online to explore which type of users will sign up).

There are a range of web-enabled sites popping up that you can use to quickly test your proposition with an available customer base. One of the earliest of these was the t-shirt fashion brand Threadless. Their key value proposition was to offer unique and cool t-shirts' design and quite quickly they realised that the choice of design was going to be the key to their success. But ordering thousands of t-shirts into stock, in the hope they had selected the most popular would be too high a risk. Their solution in the first instance was to create a web-hosted showcase page, where potential customers could view and vote on their favourite design, enabling Threadless to only order those that were voted for. The key here would then be managing the expectation of customers in terms of speed of delivery and then matching that with order fulfilment accordingly.

They were then able to add in two simple but rather clever additional functions to their original test site when they turned it into an order fulfilment site. Firstly, they realised that it was time-consuming and costly to try to create the most popular designs, so they offered a customer "design a t-shirt" competition with the best winning a prize. To determine the best they just showcased them on their original website and asked potential customers to rank them. The second development was a no brainer. By adding in ordering and purchasing capability to their site, the most popular t-shirt designs were not only ranked but were then immediately offered for purchase.

There are many sites that follow this method of consumer testing – and the barriers to entry and resource requirements are low. For instance, Amazon Mechanical Turk or MTurk can be used to crowdsource different types of testing and tasks to a distributed workforce who can perform these tasks virtually. The most sophisticated of these sites also offer routes to funding. Kickstarter originally showcased ideas for nearly completed prototype products to potential customers (prior to their manufacture). Folks were asked if they would purchase them and, if so, how much would they be prepared to pay. This soon evolved into a crowdfunding model that enabled the producers to offer "pre-sales" and thus collect revenue to take their products into production – on the promise that the customers who "bought off plan" would get a cheaper and/or exclusive first run of the goods before they were available to the wider market.

Now crowdfunding is often used at the later stages of idea testing, however we do not recommend you engage in a lengthy crowdfunding process if you are still at the problem-solution fit stage. The power of the crowd[6] – whether that be within your organisation and accessed via an intranet or outside of your organisation and accessed via the internet, should not be underestimated, but it can also lead to lost time and confusing messages if it is deployed too early or without a tight enough focus.

6 REVOLUTIONI-
ZING INNOVATION
Harhoff, D., & Lakhani,
K. R. (Eds.). (2016).
Revolutionizing
innovation: Users,
communities, and
open innovation.
MIT Press.

TEST OUR
NEW PRODUCT

SIGN UP
FOR TESTING

NAME

ADRESS

SIGNATURE

Measurement and learning are
important parts of your tests:
include actionable metrics, call
to actions and clear follow-ups
to validate your learnings.

As with the examples above, it is hugely important when you design the hypotheses tests that you remember to *build in a call to action (CTA)*. For example, if you conduct interviews with potential suspects, how do you know that they are really interested in buying this product that does not exist yet. This is tricky, you can't just rely on that potential "yes" answer. Instead, you can ask them to sign a response that states that they would be interested in trying this product before it enters the market; or perhaps they would like to partner with you to develop the product. Another CTA indicator might be the number of people that signed up to get further information about the product, etc.

Remember there is a rather large step in the customer journey from "I like that" to "I want one" to "I have purchased one"! Salespeople have known this intuitively, particularly if they were selling face-to-face but only relatively recently, with the development and now large-scale presence of web-based sales, has the research community really caught up. Based on the idea of "lead to sales" there have been extensive studies on buying habits of online customers – in turn leading to a theoretical construct of "flow"[7] with customers being in a "state of flow" when viewing a great website, that effortlessly takes them from viewing an item to making a purchase.

7 PSYCHOLOGY
OF FLOW
Csikszentmihalyi, M.
(2014). 'Toward a
psychology of opti-
mal experience'. *Flow
and the foundations
of positive psycho-
logy* (209–226).
Springer, Dordrecht.

Finally (and perhaps this is the most important part), you need to think about *your validation criteria*. How will you know that your test was successful? This is crucial to our learning and enables us to see whether we have effectively validated the hypothesis; whether we need to adjust, pivot or even abandon the solution because our hypothesis was wrong.

As we have previously mentioned and hopefully signposted, there are lots of resources available for you to design and conduct tests (not just ours – i.e. lean start-up, agile learning, business model canvas, etc.). What is crucial is to manage this exploration with a clear goal in mind!

So back to our process. As you are still in the early stages and you need to validate whether there is a real problem that your solution addresses for a group of users (problem-solution fit), you need to identify target groups of users (sometimes these are referred to as personas) and then you can conduct interviews (physical or phone meetings), observe the users and discuss with existing user communities. Or as discussed earlier you might place ads on websites like marketplace, Kickstarter or even eBay. Remember the place where you position these questioning tools must reflect the

DEFINING PERSONAS

Originally based in marketing theory, personas are usually determined in terms of a range of segmentations. These can be age-based or geographically determined, but they might also be more nuanced, such as level of education, level of user-skill, etc. Before we decided to write this book, we tried to determine its potential readers, so we sat down and sketched out a set of personas. We settled on professional (or aspiring professional) adults (or near adults), who were either employed in a company in an innovation management role or those that have an idea (innovators). We also noted our target persona to be innovators who were trying to learn how to bring their idea forward for development and funding – maybe in a partnership with an existing company. Our readers are likely to be well educated, but not necessarily in terms of qualifications or higher degrees, hence why our language style is aiming to be accessible.

nature of your solution (i.e. don't place ads on eBay if you are bringing forward an exclusively B2B proposition – Ali-Baba might be better or you can conduct short interviews at this stage with potential clients).

Remember your main goal here is to see if your solution is *a nice to have*, or *a must have*. It is all too easy to make something no one wants and there are many, many innovations that failed (we noted in an earlier chapter, a fun place to check is the "Museum of Failure" in Sweden).

One common mistake here is overselling your solution, or perhaps even trying to present your solution too early.

It is fun to watch entrepreneurs and inventors bring ideas to the mainstream that they are convinced are an elegant and necessary solution, but perhaps without identifying if there is a real problem. A particular episode of the UK show DRAGONS' DEN can be used as an analogy. The show saw an inventor bring forward a pair of leather driving gloves with the words "Drive on the Right" embroidered on the back of the glove. His solution was to remind drivers who were used to driving on the left (such as in the UK, Australia and India)

that when they were on holiday and motoring in Europe or other areas of the world that drive on the right, they must remember to keep to the right. The Dragons reacted with a combination of mirth and disdain based on their opinions that perhaps this wasn't really too much of a problem anyway and that customers were very unlikely to want to pay the purchase price for the product.

Another pitfall that we see in the *exploration* phase is that we tend to conduct tests with our existing clients or people we know and then we misinterpret results as telling us that everyone will follow suit. Also mass blind surveys are often not the best idea at this stage since you need to learn from your potential users, so if you ask them the sorts of questions that work well in a survey (ranking, comparison and short open-ended questions) the results can be so varied it is hard to ascertain exactly what they are telling you.

Once you are sure that the problem exists, you need to confirm if the market is ready for your potential offering – the *product-market fit*. You know a few users are interested and that these users are perhaps ready to pay for your solution, but the next question is how many are there? Is the market big enough and what part of this market might be accessible for you?

EXPLORATION PHASE

Exploration is as much about seeking to validate the problem as it is seeking the right solution.

Again, you don't need to test the whole solution, just the more important features of your offering – particularly the ones that drive your key assumptions. At this stage it starts to make sense to begin some simple prototyping, develop sketches to demonstrate the most important features of your solution, create a web-based landing page, create some simple videos and then engage in interviews or a further online campaigning to collect observations and evidence.

One common mistake is to spend a lot of time designing your → PROTOTYPE; falling into the misconception that you're actually designing and making your final product. Making the prototype too complicated also means you cannot determine the ─○ KEY FEATURES, to establish if they resonate with customers.

It is also easy to get carried away with the "art of the possible" when further developing prototypes, but at this stage you just need to identify the key features that customer will pay for and then once you have them locked into your proposition, you can look to iteratively improve on them (either as part of the prepare to launch phase or in a post-launch upgrade or follow-on version). This way if you hit snags when you

→ PROTOTYPE

A prototype is a sample, model or early release of a product created to test a concept or process. Prototypes are a crucial part of the design and development process. You should consider low fidelity prototypes or sometimes called preprototypes (i.e. sticky notes, sketches); Media fidelity prototypes (i.e. wireframes, online mockups) and hi-fi prototypes (nearly final products).

FOCUS ON KEY FEATURES

Question – how much functionality do you use with your new mobile phone? *Answer* – much less than is available! If we brought the idea of a smartphone to the market now, when one does not exist it is highly unlikely that customers would value all of the functionality and they would likely be unable to select which aspects are more valuable. What did you value from your first mobile phone? Was it battery life, call quality, range and coverage – or was it that if reflected your social status? What do you value now – your fitness tracker connectivity, email access, mapping and navigation software, etc.?

are approaching production, where some things are not possible, or that your resources are scarce, you can reflect back on delivering the key features that customers identified as being essential.

When your idea starts to gain more traction – perhaps you have a couple of clients lined up and need to scale up your business – you can conduct some further tests (→ TARGETED USER-SURVEYS, → A/B TESTS or even engage in → CROWDFUNDING campaign). But remember when doing this you should avoid assuming that all your clients are the same, you need to collect evidence based on numbers (collect data and not opinions!) and avoid testing too many things at once. Remember, back to our key stages of development – the *landing and growth of your business* won't normally occur at the early stages following product launch. Radical innovations tend to start slow and then gain traction rapidly later on.

Our *testing your proposition* canvas will help you to design your own tests. For each assumption, you will need to use a separate canvas. Some hypotheses might require multiple tests. Please refer to Chapter VI for the list of the most critical hypotheses to be tested.

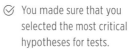

**CHECKLIST
CANVAS 6**

⊘ You made sure that you selected the most critical hypotheses for tests.

⊘ You have identified the tool that will allow you to learn the minimal knowledge needed with minimal resources.

⊘ You have identified a clear, measurable validation criterion and call to action for each test.

→ Definitions see next page

MINIMUM REQUIRED KNOWLEDGE

Build simple, quick and low-cost tests to learn the minimal knowledge needed. Ask yourself: Can I obtain the results even faster and cheaper?

Remember that there is a high risk that first ideas are not the final ones: your goal is to discard the unpromising propositions as quickly as possible.

→ TARGETED USER-SURVEYS

are online questionnaires sent to a predetermined audience to collect their feedback. The surveys should be short, straight to the point and you need to be clear what features you are testing (i.e. pricing, understand if a subscription model is good enough, colour of your products, etc.). You can use personas to target your surveys.

→ A/B TESTING

also known as split or bucket testing is often used to compare two versions of a webpage, app or email against each other to determine which one performs better. A/B testing is an experiment where two or more variants of a page are shown to users at random, and statistical analysis is used to determine which variation performs better for a given conversion goal. A/B testing can help you fine-tune your offer and find better way to engage clients.

→ CROWDFUNDING

is used to measure market demand or check if the market is ready for your idea or to introduce your product prototype while raising funds. It can be used to collect feedback from potential users while sending them your prototype or even benchmark and promote your final product. Overall, crowdfunding allows you to introduce your idea to a larger audience.

Types of testbeds.

CANVAS 6 › **TESTING YOUR PROPOSITION**

Please design tests for each hypothesis.

HYPOTHESIS TO TEST

....
....
....
....
....
....

TEST NUMBER

....

BUDGET NEEDED

☐ **Low**
less than
1k € / £ / $

☐ **Medium**
Between 1k
and 5k € / £ / $

☐ **High**
Between 5k
and 15k € / £ / $

DESCRIPTION OF YOUR TEST

What will your test consist of? How will you build it?

VALIDATION CRITERIA OF YOUR TEST

What will you measure? What minimal satisfaction level do you expect
(e.g. 20 % of my target customers want to buy my solution)?

**PLEASE SELECT THE MOST SUIT-
ABLE TOOL FOR YOUR TEST**

- INTERVIEW (ONLINE, FACE TO FACE OR CALL)
- SURVEY
- A/B OR SPLIT TESTING
- FOCUS GROUPS
- CROWDFUNDING
- MOCK-UP
- PROTOTYPE
- MODELING/SIMULATION
- ADS ONLINE
- OTHER

For example, one of the assumptions with our autonomous vehicle example was: *a user might wish to delegate 100 % of control of the vehicle within the most difficult or time-consuming parts of the drive.* This assumption raises several questions:

▷ What are the most difficult areas for the drivers?
   Is it a traffic jam, a parking manoeuvre or is it motorway boredom that drivers find hardest?
▷ Would drivers give over 100 % of control to the vehicle?
   In which conditions do these match the difficult definitions identified above?

Your first test might be to talk to at least 50 drivers about the difficulties they experience when driving and present a hypothetical offer of your partial autonomous system. You can develop a booklet, a video or a web-based landing page to supplement and bring to life your proposition. For question 1 the aim will be to collect just the drivers opinion; for question 2, your validation criterion might be that at least 80 % of the drivers agree to giving over 100 % of control of the vehicle and you would need to collect their insights and match these to the information gained in question 1.

ONLINE PLATFORMS ARE VERY EFFECTIVE WAYS TO CONNECT AND USE AS TESTBEDS BUT REMEMBER PEOPLE OFTEN BEHAVE DIFFERENTLY WHEN THEY FEEL ANONYMOUS.

Aim for simple dashboards to capture the most important objectives, learning and follow-on steps for you and your team.

Managing learning systematically

One of the most important mistakes when conducting the tests is not to record and analyse the learning correctly. Doing this accurately is important because, firstly, it creates evidence for other stakeholders; secondly, once you collect all the evidence, the decisions are easier to make. We also tend to forget the details over time and might misinterpret some of the evidence by wanting the evidence to be more positive. After all, if you are the inventor it is really hard to listen to people criticising your offering. You can use a simple → DASHBOARD to record your learning and decisions made. You can even use tools like Trello or simply to follow up on learnings.

Partial autonomous vehicles again – after interviewing 50 car users, you found out that parking appears to be difficult and time-consuming especially in busy areas or when they are in a rush. You also validate your hypothesis that drivers are happy to relinquish 100 % control during parking and they also wish to avoid having to look for available parking spaces and assess their size/suitability. With these findings, you can decide to stick to your original concept; pivot by changing your ideas based on the acquired learning (by adding in parking-space location sensing from traffic manage-

→ DASHBOARD

Dashboards are graphical user interface which often provides views of key performance indicators relevant to a particular objective or business process. Learning dashboards are great to systematically capture insights from your experiments and turn them into actions.

ment systems, GPS or size measurements using ultra-sonic sensors); or you could just discard the whole concept, deciding that our system might be too close to the current parking assist systems currently being offered on production vehicles.

Assume you have decided to continue but need to clarify your hypothesis and redesign the tests again. First, you have another open question: What solutions are available to facilitate parking? But your second question this time is about whether the driver needs to be in the car during parking? Now you pose this question to ten experts and conduct a scientific literature analysis (instead of asking 50 drivers) and you discover that retrofit parking systems are too expensive and also that the integrated, modern ones are rarely used. After several iterations and using your learning dashboard, you came up with a solution: instead of equipping cars with an integrated parking system, you can actually design one autonomous vehicle that parks all the cars within a limited zone (i.e. an airport). But then you discover a similar solution is already available. It is called Stan, the first outdoor parking robot.

Remember, you can keep, modify or discard your initial hypotheses based on your learning results.

CHECKLIST CANVAS 7

⊘ You keep your learning dashboard up to date.

⊘ For each hypothesis, you need to make a clear decision on continuing, stopping or pivoting based on your test results.

⊘ For each open question, you require clear actions to accomplish in order to find any missing knowledge.

⊘ Even if you have decided to pivot or discard your idea, you need to capitalise on the acquired knowledge.

CANVAS 7 › **PROCESS YOUR LEARNINGS SYSTEMATICALLY**
Record all your learning results and decisions.

YOUR HYPOTHESIS OR QUESTION	TEST & VALIDATION CRITERIA	MAIN LEARNINGS	NEXT STEPS & DECISION

ORGANISATIONAL STRUCTURES FOR EXPLORATION OF IDEAS

Considering the relative structural options for the exploration phase, you can probably think of many examples of MNE organisations that use their company's subsidiaries or other arms-length organisation to handle their more radical innovations. We noted Google-X and Quattro GmbH (probably the most well-known) but remember that the aim of our book is to find the best-fit option for you, based on the ideas that you are exploring, so read on.

To explore *innovation in-house*, companies will quite often establish their → INNOVATION LABS, but what do they mean by the term "lab". Well, think of a science lab: it is a place set aside for experimentation, where the environment is controlled (e.g. not influenced by external environmental conditions – it might be cold, when the outside temperature is hot and vice versa, or it might be free from dust or other particulates that would have negative effects on the experiments) but the key is that the lab environment creates the optimum conditions within which to carry out carefully controlled experiments. Think of the equipment required in these science labs (there might be microscopes, centrifuges, fume cabinets – the list goes on), but again the aim is to have on hand the machines and equipment that enables them to carry out tests simply and without delay. The labs will also often have dedicated laboratory staff, skilled in experimental design, protocol and competent in operating the equipment.

Should your company's innovation labs be any different? The answer is no. So when we get asked to run a half-day lab, in the company meeting room with a handful of staff, who all need internet passwords so they can check their emails and it must have a phone signal in case they need to "step-out to take a call". Happened to you before, right? The company wants to "sprint" to the solution and they have heard of "hacking their way" using agile methods – half a day should do it! The reality of corporate innovation labs is quite different – they might last up to three to six months or even longer, and they take staff from different backgrounds and they work continuously, ideally without interruption and engagement with the external pressures of the business, to work up hypotheses and then stress test these again and again under different conditions to de-risk their projects.

→ INNOVATION LABS

Innovation labs create a favourable exploration environment for you to test ideas in real conditions. They bring a critical perspective on the idea and help you nourish an entrepreneurial mindset. Given their expertise in testing markets in a fast way and finding product-market fit, you can save lots of time and money.

**INNOVATION LABS ARE
SHORT TERM BUT HIGHLY
SPECIALIST VEHICLES
TO TEST YOUR IDEAS.**

The labs therefore are to nurture internal ideas and also to bring ideas from the outside where entrepreneurs can work on their projects by being in-residence. In the banking sector, Credit Agricole has le Village, Société Générale created Le Plateau, NAB has NAB Labs, BPCE – Innovation Lab.

In these labs, when the ideas are created internally, the team who originated the idea has the option to work full or part-time on the project by being detached (ideally) from their day-to-day job. The *labs are therefore shielded from the pressures of everyday business*[8] and have staff employed within them who are skilled at innovation management and are able to structure workshops, discussions, interviews, pitch-decks to bring out the potential of the ideas. These lab structures are therefore not short term things and in many examples might be funded for a couple of years and whilst they need to demonstrate their success in terms of products and services taken to launch to create extended support, the establishment phase is normally written-off (or written-down) as development capital by the host company.

These labs work really well, especially given that the ideas brought into the labs are often rather immature.

8 INCUBATION MATTERS

Sedita, S. R., Apa, R., Bassetti, T., & Grandinetti, R. (2019). 'Incubation matters: Measuring the effect of business incubators on the innovation performance of start-ups'. *R&D Management*, 49(4), 439–454.

And thus, without the *protection and resources set aside in the labs,* the companies would lack the resources, headroom or management air-cover to dedicate significant time to them. Speed and accountability are important in the labs to conduct tests and record learnings.

Remember that at this stage your goal is to move fast with low resources involved.

AIR COVER FOR EXPLORATION

Having air cover for your team is to ensure that they can safely explore and experiment with the ideas knowing that you as a manager hover nearby and can provide support and protect your team if needed.

For example, Amazon has two-pizza interdisciplinary teams (the name two-pizza determines the size of the team – they can be fed with two pizzas) consisting of six to ten people to develop the idea. The teams are usually composed based on the skills required to act independently with almost zero coordination with the rest of the organisation. The teams are free to use whatever tools available to them and are driven by a single metric they all agree to follow.

But is in-house always best?

In our experience organisations that make no specific effort to separate their innovation activity from their business as usual, particularly in the exploration phase and beyond, end up quite understandably prioritising

DON'T UNDER-ESTIMATE THE IMPORTANCE OF SENIOR MANAGEMENT AIR COVER IN PARTICULAR IF YOUR LABS ARE IN-HOUSE.

the day job over developing the innovation, as we have noted before. Think of the scenario: you are leading the organisation and there is a trade-off decision to be made. Should we improve our customer service figures, reduce our delivery times, sort out that work-in-progress backlog or get to that trade event to showcase our products? These sorts of actions show hard returns for the business, so of course they will get prioritised.

Compare them to the following: Should we spend a week looking into a new idea, take staff off making the product and task them with conceiving a new one, thinking of who might buy it and who might value it – all set against metrics and calculations that are in the early stages qualitative or vague?

Whilst no one ever got fired for suggesting that they focus on innovation, the water can certainly get very hot, very quickly as you try to explain why sales figures are down, customer complaints up and on-time delivery slipped – all while the team was focussing on a new product for customers we don't have yet! This is why researchers have identified that organisations who face crises – losing customers, operating territories closing off, market failing, etc. often develop the fastest and

most radical innovations – their survival instinct kicks in. Researchers have noted, by studying the top 100 companies over a period of 50 years, that the ones that have endured have often "lurched from one crisis to another"[9].

But assume there is no real, seismic crisis. The reality is that, even with in-house innovation labs or accelerators, whilst trading is buoyant, danger appears far away and company confidence is high, the idea of separating a small team, giving them a development budget and letting them focus on things outside of the current operations is not too hard to establish. When the environment changes, however, they are the first place that managers will look to save money, retrieve their staff time or "sticking to the knitting" – a phrase we have heard quite often, even when they kill off the half-day labs.

Hence the more structurally robust models of activity, which might take longer to establish and require a higher level of commitment and attitude to risk, are often more robust and less likely to be pillaged in times of need.

9 STAGES OF BUSINESS GROWTH
Bessant, J., Phelps, B., & Adams, R. (2005). 'External knowledge: A review of the literature addressing the role of external knowledge and expertise at key stages of business growth and development'. *Advanced Institute of Management Research*, 1–78.

Another critically important decision point here is also that companies often lack the internal resources to be able to explore the ideas as fast as possible as they might need too, or they realise they lack the skills to explore new ways of working. This is when they might engage an accelerator or a company builder.

External accelerators often accommodate experience and skills for up to six months (although this can be extended), whilst also providing physical locations and equipment to enable the validation of the potential of the idea, working alongside a selection of company staff whose time is freed-up to support them. The experience provided in the accelerators might come from "entrepreneurs in residence" or key staff skilled in analysis or evaluation; they might be market experts or technology scouts. As an alternative, where companies wish to hand over their ideas for development, structures will use their own teams to do it for the corporate client and will share risks as well. These entities are called *company or venture builders* [10] (see the Barefoot or Wefound for example).

The accelerator model is grounded in the idea that firms are usually better positioned to identify business prob-

lems given their expertise and knowledge of the market, but external accelerators aim to combine this knowledge with their agile methods and enthusiasm to create a solution and explore the market in a fast and iterative way. Therefore, accelerators can create a favourable exploration environment and perform the iterative learning needed to bring the ideas forward rapidly, in real conditions with no disruption or interference from within the company's day-to-day operations. They bring a critical external perspective on the idea and an entirely different mindset. Given their expertise in testing markets in a rapid way and finding product-market fit, it might save lots of time and money for firms and help them learn a new entrepreneurial mindset from the seasoned entrepreneurs in residence.

One of the risks of this model is that as the firm, you do need to ensure that the learnings gained during the process are translated and internalised back into your company. Or you need to plan to use the accelerator model as part of your key exploration phase on an ongoing basis. Perhaps in this model you need to develop a decision structure that helps you identify which ideas you might develop with the accelerator and which ones you might choose to keep inside your organisation.

10 COMPANY BUILDERS
Köhler, R., & Baumann, O. (2015). 'Organizing for factory-like venture creation: The case of company builder incubators'. *Academy of Management Proceedings*, 2015(1), 11699.

TRULY NOVEL AND COMPLEX IDEAS WILL BE NATURALLY AVOIDED BY YOUR ORGANISATION – EXPECT IT, DON'T BE SURPRISED BY IT.

Remember that some studios often "privilege" ideas where the value is easy to reach, and they have already done something similar in the past. In this case, truly novel early stage or complex ideas will be naturally avoided. They too can suffer from the bias where they over value what they did last rather than the potential in your new idea. Also, if you recall the decision matrix in Chapter I, the key question that triggered the consideration of the accelerator model was that you had the expertise to develop the technical side of the solution but lacked the market and development experience. Therefore, you may wish to use a portfolio of accelerators – selecting different ones for different ideas.

When one of the largest banks in France launched its internal competition to identify potential start-up ideas, they decided to accelerate winning projects externally – but with a set of different accelerators. Overall, around 70 projects were accelerated during six months with different studios from all over the world, allowing the company to learn from different acceleration practices and ensure that each accelerator was selected to reflect the nature of the different ideas.

What was really interesting in this example is that the company tried to share the learning gained by their

INTRAPRENEURS
While working in your organisation, stay alert and build a relationship with potential intrapreneurs – they are your influencer work.

intrapreneurs whilst they learned in the accelerators thus creating a shared pool of knowledge. With the help of accelerators, they have developed simple weekly and monthly metrics to follow up on progress of early stage ideas and documented actions. The accelerators helped them to make objective go/no-go decisions but more importantly, they have developed a platform to capitalise on the learning for each accelerated project. This learning was provided to all other collaborators within the company.

In a similar vein, when considering rapid acceleration there is an option to work with a competitor or collaborator to create a rapid exploration model. ↪ JOINT VENTURES are often used in this context. Joint ventures are project-based activities that benefit from establishing a legal status for their activity. Their legal status enables a clear set of boundaries and working practices to be established in terms of the start conditions (including ownership of background IP), the terms and actions within the development phases (including the ownership of IP that is created in this stage) and the end state as well as how the activities in the foreground can be taken forward. This type of agreement might come into place when two similar companies wish to move

forward into exploration as partners – each contributing complimentary skills, experience, ideas and funding. Whilst more readily recognised as a way forward in the prepare for take-off or launch phases the joint venture approach enables companies to work toward collaboration without compromising themselves for diffusions in later stages.

Finally, we could consider a *start-up or spin-off* where their innovation is likely to be their main product or service. There are no issues with funding as this is undertaken at the point of incorporation (using share capital from the owners) or is set up as a programme of senior lending or other investment. All good so far, however – in the exploration phase you should be doing just that – exploring – so to form a company for this activity seems like a rather heavy handed action to explore and pan out the details of the innovation. Whilst the key resources might come from the company, with inventors being given roles as company directors or shareholders representatives, our research has shown that for some this addition of fiduciary duty works well, but for others this is problematic. (›See Chapter VII for a more detailed explanation of the pitfalls of spin-outs.) Where start-ups and spin-outs can be hugely successful

↪ JOINT VENTURE
Joint venture is a commercial enterprise undertaken jointly by two or more parties which otherwise retain their distinct identities.

IP PROTECTION

We regularly get asked about patenting and the protection it affords. The conversation normally starts with "I think I can raise just enough funds to protect it in a couple of territories" to which we respond, "how much have you got set aside to enforce an infringement?" Whilst this might seem a little overly simplistic, this is often something overlooked: the costs of enforcement can often far exceed the costs of protection, so unless you are 100 % convinced that the ownership of the patent is enough to dissuade your competitors then you must consider protection as only the first step and the first potential cost.

however is where risks are high and the industry is heavily regulated – such as pharmaceuticals or healthcare. This is also relevant for industries that rely on patent protection due to the speed of development and testing – such as aerospace for example. By vesting the IP from an early stage discovery into a separate legal entity ensures that there can be rigorous protections put in place at each stage of the exploration stage (and prepare for take-off and launch) if the idea definitely requires it; and of course if the funding can be raised to register and more importantly enforce protection of the IP. The risk in this example is spread out only as far as the initial investment from the company that originated the idea, and any lending made to the company can be called-in – if the risk is beginning to ramp up or there are serious questions about the company viability – essentially winding up the venture [11].

What is really important in the exploration phase is to consider all of these options and then make a strategic selection based on the knowns and the unknowns that you have unearthed during this phase and hopefully are set out on your canvases accordingly. «

[11] **MORE ON JOINT VENTURES**
Wallace, Robert L. (2004). *Strategic partnerships: Entrepreneur's guide to joint ventures and alliances.* Dearborn Trade Pub.

VII
CHAP

PREPARE FOR TAKE-OFF: ONBOARDING YOUR PROJECT WITHIN AND BEYOND YOUR ORGANISATION

Onboarding across your organisation and preparing a landing zone are crucial for any idea to succeed. This chapter will help you manage your development, deal with organisational and resource uncertainties and secure the future for your idea through effective communication and targeted actions.

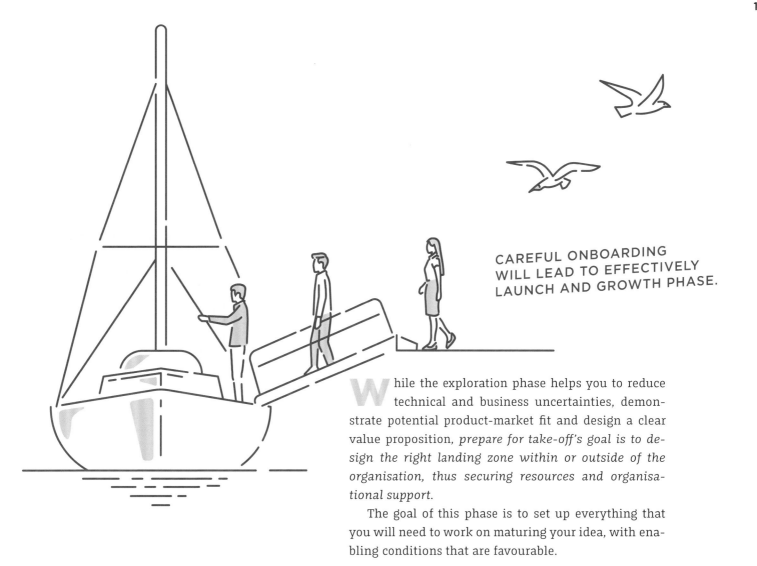

CAREFUL ONBOARDING
WILL LEAD TO EFFECTIVELY
LAUNCH AND GROWTH PHASE.

While the exploration phase helps you to reduce technical and business uncertainties, demonstrate potential product-market fit and design a clear value proposition, *prepare for take-off's goal is to design the right landing zone within or outside of the organisation, thus securing resources and organisational support.*

The goal of this phase is to set up everything that you will need to work on maturing your idea, with enabling conditions that are favourable.

As we have noted before, if your idea is radically different from your core business activities or can be seen as a competitor to any of your existing business units your project might come under fire from incumbent departments, particularly as you gain momentum toward take-off. This is perhaps where most organisations might consider creating a link with an external organisation to help them launch. The most obvious of these is to work out how to penetrate markets in the form of perhaps a marketing consultant or technology scout. Whilst we are not suggesting these activities are no longer valid, what we have seen from the most successful innovators is that they develop deeper relationships at this stage and it pays off. These are often external company builders, extensions of the joint ventures set up during exploration or new ventures focussed on launch or extensions of their skunkwork activities, but we will come to this later in the chapter.

It is good to note here: though these structural configurations are extremely important now, the truth is this: nobody is waiting for your amazing idea within the organisation. Everyone has other things to do and changing to new areas, new territories or new customers makes staff feel nervous. As Eric Ries argues in his book *(The Startup Way)*[1]:

[1] **STARTUP WAY**
Ries, E. (2017). *Making entrepreneurship a fundamental discipline of every enterprise.* CROWN, 2017.

» The hardest part for most organisations is to know what to do when the ideas have potential. «

ERIC RIES

"The hardest part for most organisations is to know what to do when the ideas have potential".

So now you really need to demonstrate the potential of your idea internally (and not just externally).

   So, to recap: You seem to have a great idea or a promising proposition to work on and you were clearly able to demonstrate its potential to both potential customers (your market tests). By now you should be confident that your solution appears to be feasible and your tests indicate that customers are interested in using it (remember our calls to actions and the evidence-based approach).

Great work so far! But if you feel like you are not at this stage yet, please go back to the discovery and exploration phases.

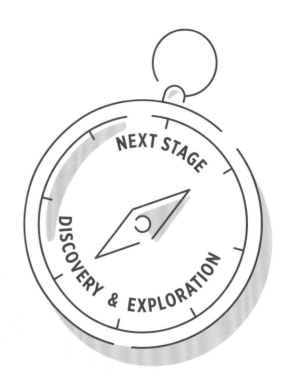

DON'T BE DISHEARTENED, BETTER TO GO BACK NOW THAN FAIL IN A MARKET.

Managing a dashboard of your exploration

Your goal at this stage is to gain support and prepare to secure necessary resources to build the more formal and more resource intensive elements of your proposition, whilst also making sure you create and share the knowledge that enables repeatable innovation processes that support your future business.

We believe that, for this, you need to start building transparency and ensure proper planning of your activities. You need to have a roadmap of tests and actions that you can communicate to any internal or external stakeholders or people becoming involved in your idea. It will help them to see how you are doing and to understand how to support you.

The main goal of this roadmap is to align your team with the main priorities and actions and also communicate your learning plan to the main stakeholders so that you can track the further steps of exploring your launch phase activities.

Whilst it might be attractive to think that you are in a position to make things more permanent, what we have learned is that it is crucial that you *do not present the design roadmap as your final plan*. It is an oppor-

ROADMAPPING

A common planning method used in practice is roadmapping; Traditional product and technology roadmaps allow organisations to map their external market situation onto internal product lineups and technology resources. These roadmaps will be useful once you prepare for launch and build your solutions.

Here we focus on development and experimentation roadmaps or dashboards to help you organise your tests from first-to-run to last; create a meaningful timeline for running your experiments and think about resources needed.

ONLY THE RESULTS FROM TESTS WILL PROVIDE YOU WITH UNARGUABLE AND TRANSPARENT DATA.

CHECKLIST
CANVAS 8

- ⊘ Verify that you have tests of different natures: technical and business.

....

- ⊘ You have built a feasible and cost-effective test roadmap.

....

- ⊘ For each learning, you checked carefully how it affects your hypothesis and your entire proposition.

tunity to enrol high-level sponsors for your initiative and gather the right people in your team (internally or through partnerships) to get funding and go further. They will want to engage with, iterate and probably re-write your roadmap and the activity of "on boarding" is hugely valuable – so be prepared to be flexible!

When working on your roadmap, the most important action is to keep track of how you are learning about your proposition (as we did in Chapter VI) and we should do this in a structured way. This enables us to check back to see the recent changes or results of experiments to establish how they relate to and challenge your initial proposition.

The *development roadmap* canvas below presents an overview of a series of business and technology tests and helps you to schedule these tests (setting target dates) and it also enables you to identify which are the most important activities you should conduct and also to confirm what your validation criteria will be. It is also important to identify and plan the resources needed for your exploration – what you will need to complete each test and therefore how long these tests will last, in terms of person/days, equipment, space, etc.

YOUR DEVELOPMENT DASHBOARD

Build simple and clear development roadmap to present your actions and make sure to keep it up to date.

Doublecheck that your tests have clear validation criteria.

Record and process learnings systematically, keep your learning dashboard up to date.

Don't be overly protective of your proposition at this stage; be rational in your assessment.

The tougher you are on your proposition today, the more credible you will be later.

CANVAS 8 › DEVELOPMENT ROADMAP

Keep track of your ongoing business and technical tests.

Choose your   ☐ Business tests* / ☐ Technical tests*

TEST NO.*	Date	TEST NO.*	Date	TEST NO.*	Date	TEST NO.*

Objective & Description: Objective & Description: Objective & Description: Objective & Description:

Validation: Validation: Validation: Validation:

ESTIMATED RESOURCES**   ESTIMATED RESOURCES**   ESTIMATED RESOURCES**   ESTIMATED RESOURCES**

Duration	Manday	Costs	Duration	Manday	Costs	Duration	Manday	Costs	Duration	Manday	Costs

* The number of tests in the roadmap depends on your proposition. The tests can be launched sequentially or in parallel.

** Estimated resources: DURATION = Time required to conduct the test. MANDAY = The equivalent of one person's working time for a day, used as a measure of how much work is required to perform the test. COST = Any external cost to realise the test.

DEVELOPING YOUR ROADMAP IS ESSENTIAL BUT REMEMBER THE FORMAT YOU SELECT MUST BE VISUAL AND SIMPLE ENOUGH TO GAIN THE SUPPORT YOU NEED.

Please see an example of the roadmap for our AI parking solution on pages 136–137.

The roadmap canvas will help you to prepare and communicate clearly your action plan to your team and important stakeholders. You can check whether you have enough resources and time to further develop your solution. At this stage, try to see if some steps can be achieved faster with less resources; check if you are focussing on the most important actions. Your first roadmap can be built based on the remaining tests designed during the exploration phase. The goal here will be to develop your solution further based on the learning achieved during the exploration phase. If you feel like the uncertainty is still too high, please go back to the sections on identification of uncertainties and designing your tests above.

Also don't be afraid to make mistakes at this stage: there might be other uncertainties that you did not take into account previously, especially if you are still facing uncertainty and the tests are still part of your learning process.[2] Based on the learnings, you can redefine the actions again (iterative learning loops).

2 **EXPERIENTIAL LEARNING**

Experiential learning is the process of learning through experience, more specifically defined as "learning through reflection on doing".

Kolb, D. (1984). *Experiential learning as the science of learning and development.* Prentice Hall.

CANVAS 8 › **DEVELOPMENT ROADMAP**

Example of business tests roadmap

Choose your   ☒ Business tests* / ☐ Technical tests*

| | 05.2020 | | | 06.2020 | | | 07.2020 | |
| | Date | | | Date | | | Date | |

TEST NO.* 1.1   **TEST NO.* 2.1**   **TEST NO.* 1.2**   **TEST NO.* 2.2**

Objective & Description:	Objective & Description:	Objective & Description:	Objective & Description:
Check if airports are interested in the autonomous parking solution.	Find an appropriate business model (renting or selling).	Is there a market for upgrading existing infrastructure or developing new parking lots and what should be an associated offer?	Make an estimation of the total available/attainable market; work on your value proposition.

Validation:	Validation:	Validation:	Validation:
At least five major international airports identified parking as a pain point and signed Memorandum of Understanding (MoU) to test the prototype (from 20).	Design a landing page and a targeted ad campaign for all the airports with a survey: collect at least 40 answers with indicated business model.	Work with partners that signed MoU to map the business scenario; further explore their pain points.	Present your value proposition to at least 30 different people within and outside your organisation; collect their feedback; adjust your proposition.

ESTIMATED RESOURCES**

Duration	Manday	Costs	Duration	Manday	Costs	Duration	Manday	Costs	Duration	Manday	Costs
60 days	30	1.000 $	50 days	20	2.000 $	40 days	20	4.000 $	40 days	30	1.000 $

* The number of tests in the roadmap depends on your proposition. The tests can be launched sequentially or in parallel.

** Estimated resources: DURATION = Time required to conduct the test. MANDAY = The equivalent of one person's working time for a day, used as a measure of how much work is required to perform the test. COST = Any external cost to realise the test.

CANVAS 8 › DEVELOPMENT ROADMAP

Example of technical tests roadmap

Choose your ☐ Business tests* / ☑ Technical tests*

	08.2020	11.2020	03.2021
	Date	Date	Date

TEST NO.* 3.1   **TEST NO.* 3.2**   **TEST NO.* 3.3**   **TEST NO.* 3.4**

Objective & Description:	Objective & Description:	Objective & Description:	Objective & Description:
Identify the best solution architecture (with min. infrastructure modifications).	Conduct security tests during the daylight and night time.	Design and conduct tests of the infrastructure required and layouts for secure data collection and processing.	Design the first real prototype in collaboration with one of the partners; test the prototype.

Validation:	Validation:	Validation:	Validation:
Collect data from different types of parking layouts; design 2–3 optimal scenarios.	Ensure that the AI solution is secure and safe (according to the relevant standards).	Tests to find gaps in security protocols are conducted with experts. The system is then reinforced.	The first prototype is installed and is running for at least three months.

ESTIMATED RESOURCES**   ESTIMATED RESOURCES**   ESTIMATED RESOURCES**   ESTIMATED RESOURCES**

Duration	Manday	Costs	Duration	Manday	Costs	Duration	Manday	Costs	Duration	Manday	Costs
80 days	60	4.000 $	120 days	100	10.000 $	100 days	80	10.000 $	250 days	200	10.000 $

* The number of tests in the roadmap depends on your proposition. The tests can be launched sequentially or in parallel.

** Estimated resources: DURATION = Time required to conduct the test. MANDAY = The equivalent of one person's working time for a day, used as a measure of how much work is required to perform the test. COST = Any external cost to realise the test.

Dealing with organisational and resource uncertainties

INNOVATION DESIGN

To generate, direct and evaluate innovations and related organisations, you engage in design activities – shift from rule-based to innovation design.

Le Masson, P., Weil, B., & Hatchuel, A. (2010). *Strategic management of innovation and design.* Cambridge University Press.

As we have noted before, when you work on radically new or breakthrough ideas, *you probably challenge your company's existing way of working* and conducting business (unless you are exploring a totally new activity or market or you are leading a start-up).

Your proposition might be too novel for the current business to comprehend and create plans and therefore you need to slowly explore what would be the best structure to use to create alignment with your current organisation and what resources you might need. You also need to think through what the competencies are that you would need to develop to fully implement this idea (both technical and non-technical) and ask yourself if you can access them easily (both internally and externally).

For example, imagine if you are a luxury champagne brand like Dom Pérignon (group LVMH). Your innovation team suggests you could gain significant market share in the low-cost, mass-produced champagne market – but wow! It might simply be against the culture of Dom

You may have the skills, expertise and knowledge for luxury yachts but are these transferrable for other boats?

POPULAR MISCONCEPTION IS BEING THE BEST AT ONE THING WILL GIVE YOU AN ADVANTAGE BUT NOT ALWAYS.

Pérignon, undermining their value offering, or ruin the concept of "terroir" that we associate with the brand. Equally the company, whilst skilled in the production, bottling and distribution of quality wine, may not have the competences or contacts to enter the lower market segments. This is perhaps a common misconception – that if you are the best at something, you must have all the skills needed to operate at a lower point on the pricing or value scale – but this is simply not true. The organisational skills and capabilities are really quite different. If nothing else, the logistics and approach to marketing will be enormously different.

So, you need to figure out whether your organisation is well positioned to bring this idea forward today or in the future. In particular, the more uncertain your idea, the more important your organisational dynamism if you want to be able to realise it. Likewise, the organisational resistance that you might encounter might also be considerable, not to mention uncertainties in the launch sector, fashion and other uncertainties.

All these factors constitute *organisational uncertainty*[3] that has to be taken into account especially when you are part of the incumbent organisation.

[3] ORGANISATIONAL AND RESOURCE UNCERTAINTIES
O'Connor, G. C., & Rice, M. P. (2013). 'A comprehensive model of uncertainty associated with radical innovation'. *Journal of Product Innovation Management*, 30, 2–18.

The solution: you need to be strategic about this – try to think who your potential internal supporters and likewise internal resistors might be. What are the expectations or concerns of the corporate-level senior managers and also the lower level operators; does your proposition align with their strategy or the way in which they normally operate and more importantly what will be the relevant organisational home for your project?

For example, in the mid-1970s the idea of using quartz watch movements to replace the existing high quality and world-renown mechanical movements of the ETA (Swatch group) just wouldn't have been accepted within the company. In fact, most of the other quality manufacturers also felt the same; the long tradition of mechanical watch manufacturing would just not stand the idea of looking into something like quartz at that time. Ironically, it was only ten years later that Swatch rescued the Swiss watch industry in the 1980s. Worried by an increase of the digital watches flooding the markets from Asia, ETA's CEO Ernst Thomke led the development of a revolutionary concept with a small team of watch engineers in secrecy. Elmar Mock and Jacques Muller [4] brought forward a complex quartz movement to reinvigorate the analogue product lines. Another uncertainty you will most likely have to deal with is *resource uncertainty*. Not forgetting that when developing ideas, you will rely on physical resources, but you will also rely heavily on non-physical, cognitive capabilities – these are your competencies. This might stimulate questions like:

- ○ *Are you sure you have the right team?*

- ○ *Will they be able to support you in delivering the first minimum viable product?*

- ○ *Do you have the right champions/sponsors for your idea onboard?*

- ○ *Can you rely on them?*

It is important to plan ahead at this stage. Your supporters might come and go so how do you ensure that your project has enough people and resources on board to support it and not tear it apart? Involving supporters with senior leadership positions is crucial at this stage so when the tough decision comes in to continue or stop the exploration there is a high probability that they understand why your solution is worth pursuing and feel more attached to it.

4 INNOVATION FACTORY
Mock, E., & Garel, G. (2018). *Innovation factory*. W. by Editions Weblaw.

For example, if you want to bring the project like Stan (›Figure 8), the robot parking assistant, forward in the BigCarCo organisation, what could be:

○ *the impact on your organisation?*

○ *the impact on the existing structure of your unit or your company?*

You will need to identify necessary competencies and think of potential transformations needed within your organisation. For example, with Stan, the business model will no longer be B2C but B2B so you would need to think of new distribution channels, promotion strategies, etc. In this model many other things might change too – perhaps you move toward a product-service transition, renting your services rather than selling your products. In this case, you need to think of key partners to bring onboard as potential clients. On our robot parking assistant model, these might be airports or train stations. Similarly, try to imagine what resources you need at this stage and what will be the best way to secure them.

CHECKLIST CANVAS 9

⊘ You have thought of existing capabilities within your organisation.

⊘ You are aware of potential transformations required to develop this solution internally.

⊘ You have a list of actions to secure resources.

ONBOARDING

Try to think of all the competencies that you might need for your project.

Try to imagine how your project impacts the existing organisational structure: Are there any threats to existing business? You need to be careful about them.

When thinking about resources needed, try to be as agile as possible: Are there any capabilities internally or externally that you can build on easily, access through partnerships?

CANVAS 9 › ONBOARDING YOUR ORGANISATION

Consider how your proposition impacts organisation and think of resource required.

IMPACT ON THE ORGANISATION

RESOURCES REQUIRED

IMPACT ON COMPETENCIES
New competencies to acquire.

....

....

....

Old competencies now obsolete.

....

....

KEY RESOURCES
Which type of resources will you need to operationalise and grow
your offer? Can you do it with fewer resources?

....

....

....

....

IMPACT ON STRUCTURE
Which type of transformation is required regarding the structure of
your organisation (partnerships, management structure, etc.)?

....

....

....

STRATEGIC ACTIONS TO SECURE RESOURCES
Which actions will you use to secure these resources?

1. ....

2. ....

3. ....

4. ....

5. ....

6. ....

Curious to see what Stan might look like at this stage?
Here is our visualisation of Stanley Robotics.

FIGURE 8 › STAN
An intelligent parking assistant from Stanley Robotics.

Setting up a communication strategy

You are now tackling one of the most challenging parts of your innovation journey: you now need to get an executive endorsement and disseminate your proposition across your organisation and beyond.

This step is as important as designing your solution and unfortunately it is where many more radical corporate innovations fail. [5] A rapidly successful innovation project typically has around 50 % of the effort dedicated to the development of the solution and 50 % devoted to communication. Your goal here is to assemble all necessary elements to deliver a successful communication strategy in order to gain internal support to move forward with your proposition.

Before designing your communication elements and polishing your pitch you need to think of the target audience:

○ *Who do you need to get onboard at this stage (internally, externally or both)?*

○ *What are your key actions?*

○ *How are you going to follow up on the progress?*

○ *Which marketing formats are you going to use at this stage (i.e. landing page, slides, flyer, working prototype)?*

Now is the time to set up your communication plan (› see canvas *setting up your communication* on p. 145).

In terms of communication plan and the format you choose to demonstrate your solution it is hugely important to present your solution in a clear way. The good news is this section probably calls on a core skill you may well enjoy and also one that you might have been good at outside of the corporate context – storytelling.

A compelling storyline is one of the most impactful ways to reach your goal and engage your colleagues and managers by pitching your proposition in a compelling manner, perhaps drawing a little on emotional connections and links to their experiences where possible.

You have to paint a picture, using words, about how your idea will solve your major customer issues, whilst telling them what you have accomplished so far and

5 VALLEY OF DEATH
Markham, S. K., & Mugge, P. C. (2015). *Traversing the valley of death: A practical guide for corporate innovation leaders.* Innovation Press.

CANVAS 10 › SETTING UP YOUR COMMUNICATION

Describe your communication plan here.

KEY PEOPLE TO GET ONBOARD	COMMUNICATION ACTIONS	PROGRESS FOLLOW UP
Who do you need to get on board to carry out your project?	Which actions will onboard the key people and your organisation (in priority order)?	How will your track the progress on your communication strategy?

**PITCHING
YOUR IDEAS**
Be ready to pitch
your proposition
to anyone in one
or several minutes
(using resources
online). Storytelling
is a scientifically-
proven way to
capture listeners'
attention.

Make your pitch
irresistible! Be really
clear on what your
product/service is
about, which group
of customers you
address and why
it is valuable.

Make sure your
presentation is
clear to anyone.

**6 FORTH
INNOVATION
METHOD**

Van Wulfen, G.
(2012). *Creating
innovative products
and services: The
FORTH innovation
method.* Gower
Publishing, Ltd.

how you plan to move forward. It is also equally important to have a set of images and mock-ups to create a background to your pitches – the technical and the financial aspects are important but so is a sketch image or other forms of visual content.

Building on this, we believe there are thousands of ways you can communicate your ideas clearly, using a range of modes or mediums to provide a way to bring your stories and pitches to life.

When it comes to designing your pitch, many tools and methods are available. We are not planning to propose a new one, but we would like you to design your pitch and connection to your ─○ COMMUNICATION PLAN. For example, our colleague Gijs van Wulfen, in his *FORTH Innovation Method* [6] suggests 30 ways to create a great pitch, including devising a short play, a poster, a video or a song. Don't forget you can have several pitches, each tuned to work with a different audience (i.e. internal sponsor, potential customer, internal venture board, external investors).

It's up to you now!

CHECKLIST

⊘ You are convinced about three key benefits of your proposition and clearly articulate them in your pitch.

⊘ You have identified a potential sponsor and key people to get onboard and your communication actions and expectations are clear.

⊘ You have practiced with at least one of your colleagues before pitching your solution.

THE BEHAVIOURAL TRAITS AND LEADERSHIP STYLES YOU EXHIBIT AS YOU TRANSITION BETWEEN EXPLORATION AND LAUNCH NEED TO BE ADJUSTED – FROM CREATIVITY TO DIRECTION, FROM INCLUSIVITY TO DELIVERY.

Organisational structures for *prepare for take-off*

During *prepare for take-off,* your goal is to start building organisational capability to support your innovations.

Remember – the more radical your idea, the bigger the challenge for your company's current expertise [7] and therefore the more effort that will be required to *prepare for take-off.*

Currently your goal should be to experiment and learn the new routines and processes that you will need to master to launch your proposition. As we noted above, these might be very different from the established routines within your organisation. Don't forget those routines were built up over many years using tried and tested methods for creating operational efficiency and driving down costs, so there are robust reasons why they are in place and – if you talk to the originators of these routines – there are robust reasons why they should stay in place! This is why it might still be too early to bring more established business units into the development of your idea at this stage.

7 DYNAMIC CAPABILITIES
King, A. A., & Tucci, C. L. (2002). 'Incumbent entry into new market niches: The role of experience and managerial choice in the creation of dynamic capabilities'. *Management Science,* 48(2), 171–186.

8 RADICAL
INNOVATION

O'Connor, G. C., &
DeMartino, R. (2006).
'Organizing for
radical innovation:
An exploratory study
of the structural
aspects of RI man-
agement systems
in large established
firms'. *Journal of
Product Innovation
Management*, 23(6),
475–497.

9 AMBIDEXTROUS
LEADERSHIP

Rosing, K., Frese, M.,
& Bausch, A. (2011).
'Explaining the
heterogeneity of the
leadership innovation
relationship: Ambi-
dextrous leadership'.
*The Leadership
Quarterly*, 22(5),
956–974.

Prior research and empirical study stresses that to commercialise radical innovations, *loosely coupled and stand-alone organisational units should be assembled*[8], which will help to explore appropriate business models and processes, but without meeting the resistance to these explorations that might hamper your develop-ment long term. The reason for this is that exploration and exploitation require different sets of skills and ca-pabilities. The ability to lead the exploration phase and the ability to balance both explore and exploit might be required at this stage. This is often defined as *ambidex-trous leadership*[9]. Some organisations prefer to avoid the conflict and separate explore and exploit units. (But Beware! Think of translating the activity between these units – this is not trivial, and this is also where the in-novation potential often gets lost.) The good thing is we are still in the prepare for take-off phase so you can think how and where the developed capability should be developed or translated.

In our model for *internal innovation labs or accelera-tors*, developing projects have access to the assets and resources of the main organisation, yet we note that these interfaces with the mainstream activities can also be the undoing of the project. Thus we reach a par-

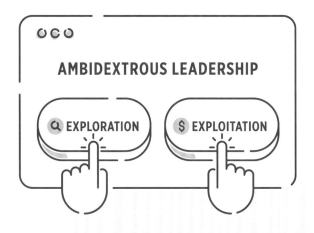

AMBIDEXTROUS LEADERSHIP

EXPLORATION   EXPLOITATION

IT CAN FEEL A BIT LIKE JUGGLING, OR PATTING YOUR HEAD WHILST RUBBING YOUR STOMACH – BUT STICK WITH IT – IT GETS EASIER.

adox – in the in-house models it is hugely important to stay close to the main organisation (as they deploy resources and govern outcomes) and they can also communicate details about your project and help you to develop your commercial activities (such as sales, marketing, distribution, after-sales). But they can also spell the end for your idea.

Balancing this tension can be tricky – and this is why organisations create wider degrees of separation for their activity at this stage, more than at any other. Thus, creating a degree of separation and conducting this work as a standalone activity (as with skunkworks). In this model, physical separation from your company can provide more freedom, agility and the ability for you to build a new and different culture. However there is also a compromise: if the ultimate goal is to develop the solution with the main company, a complete separation might not be wise since you will need to translate the results within your organisation and build new competencies gradually (balancing exploration versus exploitation as indicated above).

Certainly the most renowned skunkworks is the one created by Lockheed Martin in the 1950s, but more

recently GOOGLE X and MICROSOFT RESEARCH fit the definition of a skunkworks model, as their teams work in secrecy to develop new ideas. What is important here is that teams are isolated from the core business; there is almost no day-to-day management imposed nor is there mainstream alignment with the main organisation's capabilities. It is this freedom and diverse skill-base inside the skunkworks that helps it elaborate and implement new ideas.

One of the most successful examples of skunkworks is AMAZON'S LAB 126, located in Silicon Valley, away from the company's main headquarters in Seattle. Since its establishment in 2004, the team has been able to design and engineer devices like Fire tablets, Kindle e-readers, Amazon Fire TV, Amazon Echo and much more.

When conducting *discovery, exploration* and *prepare for take-off* in a semi-external structure like Amazon Lab 126, *one key consideration* is to establish at which stage the skunkworks should begin to interact with the host organisation. You can perhaps think of it as an API: How will you design the interface for your solution to communicate with the main platform? Therefore, establishing suitable interfaces with the main organisation is important both for the purposes of your project

EXPLORATION – EXPLOITATION TRADE-OFF

This is often the "million dollar" challenge – the exploitation pays the bills today and exploration the bills tomorrow – but its hard to take your attention off of today's problems to make time!

**"OFF THE SHELF"
SERVICES**

The simplest way
to set up a company
is to use an "off
the shelf" service.
Service providers set
up companies and
then sell them on,
to be re-purposed
and operated. It
is important to
remember though,
once you set it up
you have to keep it
going and that can be
time consuming and
tiresome if you are
struggling with your
innovation too.

and perhaps, to share lessons learned with other business units and thus we see that other forms of separation are evident.

Instead of skunkworks models, organisations might go to a greater and less flexible degree of separation and *spin-out* a new company as a subsidiary of the main organisation – the benefits of autonomy are present in the subsidiary – where new company appointments can sit alongside staff who have moved out of the main organisation (on a full-time or partial appointment basis) and can focus specifically on the new project. The fundamental downside of these models is two-fold:

1 — Ownership and IP

Creating a new company, whilst a relatively simple legal exercise, can create intense tensions at the board-level with executives questioning the motives of the staff trying to establish the spin-out. Asset ownership, access and recovery can also be a minefield. Negotiations around share ownership and foreground IP can also prove testing – with the board considering it better to own 100 % of the idea (as they do in the other structural models apart from *joint venture* and *company builder*)

rather than a watered-down share if, or when, the spin-out begins to grow and requires additional investment. The stark reality here is often that the parent company might not bring the product to market without the space and freedom that the spin-out provides and thus the discussion is really around owning a 100 % of nothing (if the idea never makes it to launch) or whether it is better to own a smaller share of a successful, radical innovation.

2 — Employee management

The other issue is how existing staff feel about working within a spin-out in terms of their fiduciary duties and how these might resolve when considering their own long-term employment, particularly if their directors role is part of a temporary secondment, or partial role on the board of the spin-out. In the commercial model of spin-out it becomes hard to balance internal tensions between doing right by the spin-out (as your fiduciary duty legally dictates) and also doing the right thing by your previous (or current) employer – especially if decisions present themselves that compromise one party or another. These tensions can lead to decision paralysis – slowing the development process and negating

THE COMPANY BUILDER IS A POWERFUL MODEL… AS YOU CAN WORK ALONGSIDE INNOVATION PROFESSIONALS AND COMPANY STAFF, ALL FOCUSSED ON MAKING THE INNOVATION SUCCESSFUL.

the degree of flexibility and agility sought out from the spin-out model in the first place.

As a resolution to these issues, to some extent is the *company builder* model. This model is powerful as it allows the key staff from the main organisation to work alongside specialist innovation professionals and company professionals, who are used to working with these tensions and will have strategies and resolutions in place to develop the new product at speed. Their terms and conditions will also be created to sidestep many of the issues identified when bringing staff from the main organisation and enabling them to work effectively in the company builder model. The reality is that every company builder programme is slightly different and structured slightly differently accordingly – thus it is important to explore each model carefully, with due diligence performed to ensure their model of company builder works for your organisation and your proposition. One successful example we have come across is ENGIE, and the company builder provision called Wefound. Wefound develop and test ideas for ENGIE and also for other partners independently, focussing in particular on creating "in-house" innovation activity based on applying a start-up model.

As the founder of Wefound, Gilles Debuchy points out:

> *"With our first partner, Engie, we have been able to identify a dozen potential start-ups that were compatible with the company's pre-defined strategic goals. We then went through a phase of creation and launch of those start-ups for which the timing seemed most favourable. The first has been launched in December 2018: Greenmove, which democratizes access to electric mobility".*
> GILLES DEBUCHY

→ COOPETITION
Coopetition is where competitors work collaboratively to develop a new product, only to compete for market share with each other once the product is launched.

Joint ventures (JV) are a beneficial alternative that enable companies to allocate and "ring fence" specific resources to the new proposition, bringing forward a partner company that can also enter into the JV, and in turn bring a different set of resources toward the development of the final proposition.

One powerful example of this JV-style development between incumbent companies is the small "city car" launched in the late 2000s. The fundamental design, specification and manufacture of the vehicle took ide-

COOPETITION MIGHT SEEM ODD – TO CO-OPERATE WITH YOUR COMPETITORS BUT ACTUALLY THERE ARE MORE EXAMPLES OF THIS PRACTICE IN EVERYDAY LIFE THAN YOU REALISE.

as, components and manufacturing from Toyota, Citroen and Peugeot (quickly noted by the motor trade as odd bedpartners) to create a platform model – that was then configured by each company during the final stages of manufacturing and sold as the Toyota Aygo, Citroen 1 and Peugeot 107 accordingly.

This form of → COOPETITION is interesting in itself. Whilst uncommon in the motor industry (where the dominant model for many years was acquisition) the model has been hugely successful in other areas – take the restaurant and tourism industry. Often an area of a town will become a restaurant district and the owners are quick to realise if you jointly market the area, encourage transport links to the area, fund security and clean up, etc. then each business wins in the long run. They collaborate to gain footfall and then compete to win each customer into their establishment accordingly.

The key differentiator here, and therefore the decision around which model to adopt centres around your key goal for each phase.

For example, when preparing for take-off within your in-house innovation lab, the common mistake is to use the same organisational structure and goals from the exploration phase for the activities related to the prepare for take-off phase. Why? Well if in the exploration phase your goal is to kill the idea as fast as possible to avoid investing in useless ideas, this is certainly not the goal in the prepare for take-off phase. Now you want to nurture and build your capabilities in further deploying the idea, securing resources and support (you are indeed transitioning from exploration to exploitation). The mindset and the dynamics of exploration are very different – and thus the management and therefore their role in the innovation lab must change.

One example that brought this home was during a discussion with a high-ranked military commander – they talked about a transition they have to make between a hierarchy and a heterarchy. When they set up a mission control centre – the start-up phase of a campaign or mission – they bring together senior ranks from different backgrounds (weapons, communications, logistics, etc.) all under the control of the senior officer. Their first job is to plan the mission and then to set up a command control system accordingly – to bring the operational part of the mission to life. In this set up phase, the commander talked of wanting lots of opinions, vibrant discussions and a culture where, regardless of

ACQUISITIONS

Large MNEs have dominated the car industry, buying up competitor marques and brands as their market share faltered – SAABs acquisition by General Motors springs to minds, or BMWs acquisition of Land Rover before releasing it to create Jaguar Land Rover for example.

rank, each officer's contribution was valid. Decisions would be based where possible on evidence, but the experiences of the officers were crucial with discussions informal and relaxed. They referred to this as creating a heterarchy. However, they were very clear that – once the mission commenced – there was no place in mission control for any part of this and the hierarchy would dominate at this stage. The hierarchy of rank, of correct use of salutation and respect and the expectation that orders were to be carried out to the letter without discussion and delay, would reassert itself.

Similarly, if you reflect on the key teachings in project management, a similar shift in goals and therefore culture is noted. In the concept, feasibility and outline design phases variety, potential solutions and creative discussion are definitely what is required. The goal therefore is to explore potential solutions and arrive at the best-fit solution. When the permissions, budget and detailed design are in place and the focus turns to implementation, the goals change considerably and so does the culture[10] – the focus is now very much on time, money and quality as well as control over any variances that might cause either of these metrics to be exceeded.

In practice, in terms of innovation, there is no right way to do something and thus we very much urge you to reflect on this question. We suggest if you conduct discovery and exploration activity in-house or at least close to home, there should not be an automatic expectation that you must continue with this format for the prepare for take-off phase.

It is an important point so let us try to explain it with reference to an example. In the banking industry example described in Chapter V, the majority of the projects in the example portfolio focussed on the exploration phase, stopping at that point. However, for the ones that proceeded some continued into *prepare for take-off* in-house and some with external accelerators. In one of the examples a team of employees joined an accelerator for six months to explore the idea of launching services for SMEs, artists, craftsmen, freelancers and start-ups. Based on the exploration conducted within the accelerator, the company decided to spin-out a new "digital" bank that belongs 100% to the company and is dedicated entirely to early-stage professionals. The products are now fully deployed, and the offer is available on the market. The degree of separation achieved in the accelerator enabled the end-product to be highly

10 FEARLESS ORGANISATION

For a practical guide for creating cultures, see

Edmondson, A. C. (2018). The fearless organization: *Creating psychological safety in the workplace for learning, innovation and growth*. John Wiley & Sons.

BY UNDERSTANDING WHAT TRAVELERS VALUED MOST IN CAR SHARE, THE COMPANY COULD BRING THESE BENEFITS TO THEIR BUS NETWORK.

personalised to the needs of artisans, micro-companies and professionals.

A second example: when a French transportation company was exploring different micro-transit solutions, they came up with the idea of ridesharing to work. As an internal idea it was developed and then deployed in the UK entirely within the company – but in one of their dedicated business units focussed on collecting, collating and analysing data.

The novelty of the project was to use flexible rerouting provisions to avoid traffic, for people who were ridesharing. The proposition therefore was that sharing provided a quicker journey as well as economies of sharing transport costs, etc. The pilot project, launched in the city of Bristol in 2016 created more than 40,000 passenger trips, covering 210,000 kilometres over two years and receiving an average of 4.9 out of 5 ratings from customers. The pilot was closed in 2018 and the learning of how much users valued speed and cost-savings in taking their journeys was used to design and develop the new Metrobus Rapid Transit System. The pilot project (that was initially planned for six months) lasted for more than two years and created invaluable learning on how to operate micro-transit transport

ON ORGANISATIO-NAL STRUCTURES

One way to compare organisational struc- tures is to sketch out the process flow for your innovation in each structure and then compare – this way you can decide if speed is more critical than onboarding for aftersales, or if confidentiality and secrecy are more vital than access to internal development funds?

solutions. The next step for them will be to integrate the solution as a complement not competitor to the wider public transport system.

Overall, when selecting your organisational structure, you need to think of what capability you need to develop; the way you are going to balance between exploration activity and the mainstream processes of your organisation. Try to think which processes and capabilities of your organisation will be helpful for your proposition and which ones are going to problematic.

Don't forget, onboarding and communication activities are crucial to secure people who will support you and understand what you are doing even if you will be working externally with a company builder.

Imagine what is the ideal landing zone for your project and try to think how to accomplish this, whilst also ensuring you can achieve your desired milestones. «

VISUALISING YOUR IDEAL LANDING ZONE MIGHT SEEM ABSTRACT BUT THINK ABOUT WHAT THE CURRENT LANDSCAPE LOOKS LIKE OFTEN HELPS YOU TO START – YOU COULD USE A SIMPLE FRAMEWORK LIKE MCKINSEY'S 7S OR THE WIDELY USED PESTEL MODEL. EACH HELPS YOU EXPLORE VARIOUS DIMENSIONS OF THE LANDING ZONE AND IDENTIFIES WHAT YOU CAN CHANGE, AND WHAT YOU CAN'T.

CHAP

ASSESSING READINESS FOR LANDING: THE APPROPRIATION OF RADICAL INNOVATIONS

This chapter will bring you towards the end of the development phase and help manage the trade-offs between exploration and exploitation. You will assess whether you are ready to launch your product and consider again the possible structures you can use to do it.

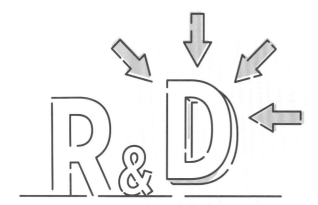

MOST PEOPLE UNDERSTAND THE RESEARCH ASPECT BUT WHAT HAPPENS IN DEVELOPMENT CAN BE MORE CONFUSING – WHICH IS WHY IT IS PART OF THE FUZZY FRONT-END OF INNOVATION.

Congratulations! You are almost there – or at least almost ready to launch. Your journey has led you to a *Key Milestone* that is common to any innovation project. This is the moment where the company *decides officially to finance and launch a new product, service or technology.*

This is also the moment where you would often be entering into the latter and more formal process of new product development, or the latter phases of the "stage gate" or waterfall process of development; in simple terms it corresponds most of the time to the D in R&D. If you come from a technical background this will correspond to the later stages of the Technology Readiness Level processes – focussed on development and commercialisation. If you refer more to New Product Development, we are at the end of the Fuzzy Front End.

First off all, you will need to check what the current process is for developing and launching new products or services within your organisation (if you are doing it internally). Based on your work with your sponsors and innovation managers, you have a clear idea if you will need to go through the formal processes (like gate reviews; go/no-go decisions) or not.

**IMPORTANCE
OF EXECUTION**

Execution is as important as discovery or exploration: average ideas could be worth millions if executed well, while brilliant ones can flop due to poor execution. For more, check: Sivers, D. (2015). *Anything you want: 40 lessons for a new kind of entrepreneur.* Penguin.

Now you might be thinking – hold on; I thought we would be launching independently or at best we might be close to the launch by now. The reality here is that most organisations will have some form of investment system within which your proposition will now have to fit – in order for the other departments to be able to make sense of the role that they will, or will not, be required to play in the activity. Remember our banking examples: even though these were online offerings, delivered by a new department who were targeting new customers, there would still be an operational overlap – and thus checks and balances made on the new innovation in order for it to operate in the customer services system, be on the right side of regulations, have been checked for money laundering and other legislation compliance. So even when putting this activity in a skunkworks or developing it in an accelerator these interactions would still be essential.

Think about a Land Rover Special Vehicle (Land Rover's legendary bespoke and low volume development and production team). They can design, build and despatch their own vehicles directly to customers, so they had a huge degree of flexibility, autonomy and access to their customers – but at the end of the day their vehicles were still Land Rovers and thus needed to be warrantied, maintained and serviced by the dealer network and replacement parts supplied by the marque – at least for a reasonable period of time before aftermarket competition kicked in.

In this example your proposition has to fit operational and end-user requirements provided by your organisation and you would need to have a clear idea of resources required, partnership to put in place, timeframe, costs, etc. to make this happen (you can go back to Chapter VII to work on your organisational and resource uncertainties).

Don't underestimate this activity as this phase can be tricky to manoeuvre and you will need to have support from champions within your organisation as effectively, you are trying to dismantle their customer interface but you are also trying to dismantle your interface, built by you to protect and nurture your idea and check whether your company is ready for it. It is the final step where your proposition can falter, or where it becomes part of your company's product or service offerings. Now don't get too relaxed: there is a whole world of market failure to worry about, but at this stage it is the final part of buy-in.

INNOVATING IS ALSO ABOUT EXECUTING SOMETHING WELL AND BETTER THAN YOUR COMPETITORS.

In this chapter we will not be able to cover the specificity of every single organisation when it comes to deploying their innovative solutions but there is one specific structural model we have not mentioned thus far which often arises out of the results of the prepare for take-off phase – where the organisation decides to launch the product or service outside of their brand and thus their organisation.

As an example, when EnBW, a company that provides German households with moderately-priced gas and electricity supplies came up with their new product, the OilFox, they had some key decisions to make in terms of post-launch activities. The OilFox is a measuring device which is screwed directly onto the oil tank and allows continuous measurement of the level of the oil using ultrasound. The monitor bounces a signal off the reflective surface of the contents – thus the product could be beneficial for many other markets (outside of oil and gas) but it would also be useful for their competitors too. The company realised quite quickly that developing it internally would decrease its potential market size and so they decided to launch an entirely independent company to commercialise the solution.

Deciding on the suitable organisational form for your business is a strategic decision that you and your sponsors will have to make. Hopefully, your work on the roadmap and communication plan allowed you to build evidence on what would be the best approach. You might consider going back if you feel like these areas are not properly explored.

Our goal in this last chapter is to help you check whether you are ready for the development or exploitation

INNOVATION ADOPTION

We hope you have the idea that going back at this stage, and indeed any stage of our process, can seem hard to reconcile, but from experience the innovations that ensure they are ready, often benefit considerably – particularly if they are more radical. Microsoft can afford to let users "snag" the bugs out of their new operating systems – but would you have adopted an incomplete product if it was the first time you had seen it?

**ATTITUDE
TO RISKS**

When is enough
evidence enough?
It is worth thinking
about your per-
sonality type. It is
commonly stated that
"Entrepreneurs will
risk their shirt on a
venture, about which
they understand just
enough to go for it".
But the reality isn't
really that romantic –
successful, repeat
entrepreneurs make
careful judgements
based on information
and evaluation – your
innovations need to
be the same. It might
not be your shirt you
are risking, just your
reputation, but re-
member it took years
to build and seconds
to tarnish.

phase in general and give you some insights on how to address formal review processes in case you might have to deal with one.

To succeed in the review process (if you will have one), you normally need a validated concept and as much evidence as you can offer to support your claim. The following *Assessing readiness for landing* canvas indicates the strength of the business case and aims to identify how achievable your proposition is. It is aimed at enabling managers to make informed decisions, with the lowest possible level of risks.

Remember if you are not able to pass the review, it does not necessarily mean that your project isn't worth launching, just that you might need to come back to one or more of the canvases and tackle some of the challenges in depth. Or perhaps, you need to work harder to onboard your organisation so they truly grasp the potential of this idea. Well, it can happen that after all your efforts the company (for many reasons) is not ready to allocate resources for your solution. In this case, you can see if you can negotiate building a company on your own as a spin-off.

**CHECKLIST
CANVAS 11**

- ⊘ If your business opportunity and feasibility assessments bring you to the green zone, you can start preparing for the landing phase.

- ⊘ Check if you have identified a clear sponsor internally or you are backed by the organisation to develop externally.

- ⊘ Perhaps ask colleagues to review your proposal in order to check if something is missing.

CANVAS 11.1 › **ASSESSING READINESS FOR LANDING**

Evaluate if your proposition is mature enough for landing.

BUSINESS OPPORTUNITY

For each column please indicate where you offer stands.

CRITERIA		0		1		2		3	
ADDED VALUE	Added value potential?	None	☐	Low	☐	Moderate	☐	High	☐
MARKET SIZE	Value of market and potential market share	Low market, small share	☐	Low market, large share	☐	High market, small share	☐	High market, large share	☐
POTENTIAL TO SCALE	Growth capacity within the target business model	Low/None	☐	Medium	☐	High	☐	Very high	☐
COMPETITIVE ADVANTAGE	Performance against competition	None	☐	Small	☐	Medium	☐	Big	☐
RETURN ON INVESTMENT	Can development cost be recovered?	No	☐	Long term	☐	Medium term	☐	Short term	☐

ADD UP YOUR BUSINESS OPPORTUNITY SCORE. ☐

CANVAS 11.2 › ASSESSING READINESS FOR LANDING

Evaluate if your proposition is mature enough for landing.

FEASIBILITY

For each column please indicate where you offer stands and the level of challenges associated with the development.

CRITERIA		0		1		2		3	
COMPLEXITY	Number of components, quality assurance	High	☐	Challenging	☐	Moderate	☐	Simple, easy	☐
COMPETENCIES	In-house knowledge expertise	None	☐	Limited/low in-house	☐	In-house capability	☐	High level, in-house	☐
SUPPLY CHAIN	Strength of the supply chain	No supply chain at present	☐	New supplier	☐	Existing – sole supply	☐	Existing – choice	☐
RESOURCE COMMITMENT	Man / hours required	High	☐	Medium	☐	Low	☐	High	☐
TIME	Time to market	Long	☐	Medium	☐	Short	☐	Long	☐

ADD UP YOUR FEASIBILITY SCORE.   ☐

CANVAS 11.3 › ASSESSING READINESS FOR LANDING

Are you in the blue area? Based on your opportunity and feasibility assessments, determine where your proposition is located on his diagram.

ADD UP THE TABLE RANKING INDEPENDENTLY

11.1 → BUSINESS OPPORTUNITY SCORE

11.2 → FEASIBILITY SCORE

SCORE	RANK
0 TO 3	1
4 TO 6	2
7 TO 9	3
10 TO 12	4
13 TO 15	5

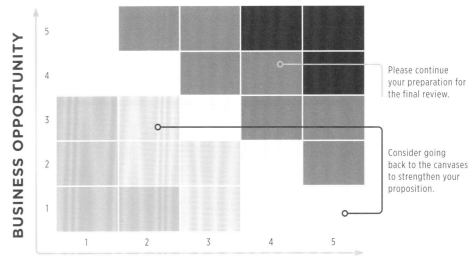

Please continue your preparation for the final review.

Consider going back to the canvases to strengthen your proposition.

WHAT NOW?

If you are in the light blue/blue, please continue your preparation for the Gate Review. If not, please see whether it is a business opportunity or technical effort that need to be enhanced (or both). Go back to the corresponding challenges in the Innovation Toolkit to strengthen your proposition.

PART 3

CONCLUSION:
HOW TO ENSURE A CULTURE OF COHERENT INNOVATION PORTFOLIO MANAGEMENT WITHIN YOUR ORGANISATION

CHAP

LOOKING FORWARD

Our concluding Part 3 will offer you some reflections on the importance of long-term thinking, portfolio management and organisational culture.

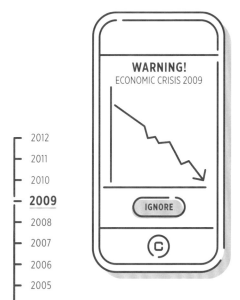

THE FUTURE IS COMING,
IF YOU CAN ALLOCATE AT
LEAST 1% OF YOUR TIME
TO CONSIDER THE FUTURE.

Innovation often happens in difficult and uncertain times, often when there simply isn't a "do nothing" option, and we have also noted before, that it comes with its own paradox: How can you ensure that your company manages its day-to-day operations while also developing readiness for the future.

The good news is there are numerous examples of companies delivering successful breakthroughs during difficult times. Just look at Apple: their iPhone 3G was launched during the economic crisis in 2009. We urge you to think, even if the current situation is difficult and you are putting 99% of your effort and resources into sustaining the short term, perhaps you can still allocate 1% to look into the future and explore possibilities for your business. And it doesn't need to be undertaken alone – as we have seen in this book there are many organisational structures that you might consider that release just a little of the day-to-day operational pressures and create a space to work on the new things. What we are trying to say is absolutely focus on the day-to-day, but spare a little time for moonshot thinking and more importantly for some moonshot doing!

1 INNOVATION PORTFOLIO

Kokshagina, O., Le Masson, P., Weil, B., & Cogez, P. (2016). 'Portfolio management in double unknown situations: Technological platforms and the role of cross-application managers'. *Creativity and Innovation Management*, 25(2).

PORTFOLIO MANAGEMENT

You can view portfolio management a little like balancing a spread bet – a little money where there is large risk, a little more where there is less risk. If the high risk pays out – great. If not then you can fall back on the lower but more reliable returns.

We are not alone in thinking *the portfolio approach*[1] *is the key to it*. As a manager responsible for innovation within the company or a CEO, don't think in terms of one idea, solution, proposition – think about a portfolio. How can you spread your resources across a range of activities, some simple and likely to return reliable but small yields and some more complex but likely to return riskier but higher yields (only later) and perhaps equally importantly: How can you manage the learning you get from each of the different projects?

From our experience, your core improvements (often incremental innovations) will be 60 % of the overall innovation portfolio; 30 % will be your stretch projects, but that have relatively low uncertainty (operating at the edge of your current activity and markets) and 10 % will be highly exploratory projects. Is this the case within your organisation? We bet it isn't!

Going back to various organisational structures discussed in the book: How might they each support this portfolio? Ideally you would have an innovation director or CIO who is overseeing the whole portfolio – and who has a visibility across all the various structures that company is experimenting with in terms of inno-

MOST IMPORTANTLY, DON'T UNDERMINE YOUR CORE ACTIVITIES, BUT SPARE A LITTLE TIME FOR MOONSHOT THINKING AND MOONSHOT DOING!

vation efforts. Hopefully you have seen that one size doesn't have to fit all – and that some ideas can be housed internally, whilst others can be taken into different structures and we suggest this is the most complex dimension of your book to understand – it is often just *"horses for courses"*, so to speak.

If this is the case, you will be managing collaborations with accelerators, company builders, deciding whether skunkworks are appropriate or whether to manage the idea internally. This will depend on the nature of the ideas, the stage of maturity, the degree of uncertainty, etc. – all the things we have tried to reduce the uncertainty of in using our canvases.

Overseeing all the innovation initiatives within the company is a great way to progress an innovation portfolio. It offers the ability to aggregate results (rather than ignoring the incremental ones or just badging these as operational improvements) and show the risks, the likelihood of failure and the investments made as a big picture. It is also enormously important in terms of processing the learning from these initiatives. Sadly, in reality, it happens rarely. We observe many fragmented initiatives at the different levels of the organisation, that are often disconnected and where there is no sharing of good practices or collective learning from failure across the organisation.

One tip here: making the process of learning, realisation and action intentionally separate might be helpful, as people are often capable of realising learning from failure – but then fail to do anything different the next time, to act on this learning. This is referred to by knowledge-orientated scholars as single versus double-loop learning[2], but it really became clear what this meant practically when conducting an innovation workshop with a team of senior leaders from a police force. As a result of the workshop discussion they decided to separate the phase of *lessons learned* into two distinct steps – the first is *lessons realised* and the second is *lessons applied*. When discussing the process they followed when attending and dealing with serious motor-vehicle collisions, they noted from their previous post-incident reports that they were very good at identifying ways to improve the process, but then lacked the time and resources to implement changes to procedures and training to embed them. By separating the phases into lesson realised and lesson applied they could take a strategic decision to focus on the most important lesson from each incident (by ranking them

2 **DOUBLE-LOOP LEARNING**
Argyris, C., 1977. 'Double loop learning in organizations'. *Harvard Business Review*, 55(5), 115–125.

**EXPLORATION –
EXPLOITATION
TRADE-OFF**

The exploration-
exploitation trade-off
is a well-known prob-
lem that occurs when
we have to repeated-
ly make a choice and
where the pay-offs
are uncertain. This
well known dilemma
for a decision-making
system between
repeating decisions
that have worked
well so far (exploit)
or to make novel
decisions, hoping to
gain even greater
rewards (explore).

For more details,
please refer to the
seminal work of
March, J. G. (1991).
'Exploration and
exploitation in orga-
nisational learning'.
Organization Science,
2(1), 71–87.

in the post-incident report) and then they could allocate resource to action a change from just this one. They
were confident this piecemeal approach would lead to a
greater set of changes when considered over a period of
time and compared to their current system.

*Moving on – another important note is that if you are
the manager responsible for innovation within the firm,
you need to manage the interfaces between different
departments and also ensure that there are working
trade-offs between exploration and exploitation activities.*

Now imagine a company's marketing department or-
ganises a hackathon, engaging with students to attract new top-level talent and improve the profile and
standing of the company; at the same time the innovation department has launched an internal innovation
contest to collect ideas for the discovery phase. The
company's internal accelerator is building their sprint
to accommodate new external start-ups and perhaps,
identify some potential intrapreneurs with good ideas.
All these departments focus on delivering their KPIs but
without coordination many of these initiatives will not
go beyond the exploration phase.

Perhaps ask yourself:

○ *Do you know how big your
  innovation portfolio is?*

○ *How many and which type of
  organisational structures are involved?*

○ *Do you know how balanced these
  projects are across the core, periphery
  or breakthrough markets?*

○ *What is the balance between
  incremental and radical?*

○ *How are these projects/ideas balanced
  across stages of innovation exploration:
  discovery, exploration, prepare for take-
  off and of course launch?*

INNOVATION IS LESS EXCLUSIVE WHEN BUILT INTO THE IDENTITY, OR THE DNA OF THE FIRM.

We have learned that success requires mastering all three phases: *discovery, exploration* and *prepare for take-off.* We have also learned that what is important here is to gradually mature your innovation capabilities over time and across structures, projects and phases.

And finally, one of the critical aspects to help nurture innovation within companies is all about making innovation less exclusive by building it into the identity, or the DNA of the firm. There are definitely no reasons why you should not innovate every day. There is also no reason why anyone and everyone (no matter their role in the organisation) is not capable of coming up with new and (most importantly) good ideas. To enable this, we must not just *focus on projects but also on habits and routines among our employees to nurture an innovative culture within our organisation.*

Companies such as HubSpot, for example, have their own cultural manifestoes, shared with all the employees and also used to dictate the recruitment modes, in the hope of finding the most suitable candidates. We have also noted how GE trained more than 60,000 employees in lean start-up and developing different habits around innovation is part of their culture. Other firms

WORKPLACE ATTITUDE TO INNOVATION

When firms first started trying to stimulate innovation, there was considerable focus on the physical layout and furnishings of "innovative spaces". Recent research suggest this is important but cannot be isolated from the workplace attitudes to innovation. It is like the boss with the open door policy – who shouts as you approach the door! Having brightly painted rooms and soft furnishings won't change the behaviour of staff overnight!

are building small hacks for their employees as well. For example, Asana has no-meeting days, HubSpot has unlimited free books, Amazon has an empty chair policy during the meetings or "our memo from the future", Stim introduces green light principle to encourage productive work in the open office.

START-UP MINDSET
The purpose of "fail fast, fail often and act quickly" is not to fail, but to be iterative. To succeed, we must be open to failure – sure – but the intention is to ensure we are learning from our mistakes as we tweak, reset, and then restart if necessary.

These small hacks will not revolutionise the way your company deals with innovation, but they will gradually support the development of skills necessary for innovation to be successful, for example, by being:

○ *curious;*

○ *evidence and data driven;*

○ *customer obsessed;*

○ *collaborative;*

○ *super-comfortable with ambiguity and the unknown;*

○ *and accepting of risks and of failure.*

Try to think:

○ *Which type of behaviour needs to be encouraged to be more successful in dealing with innovation portfolio (both for innovators and for decision makers)?*

○ *What are existing habits or routines in the organisation that prevent that behaviour?*

○ *What do you need to do to enable behavioural change?*

Reflecting back on one of our early examples – when the banking company's top executives became involved as sponsors and mentors for the new start-ups, the innovation team was concerned about the executives lack of experience in the start-up mindset of "fail fast, fail often and act quickly". To try to combat this issue the team secured agreement for a mandatory training session for the executives, delivered by one of the external accelerator partners, to introduce the principles of validated learnings, minimal viable products, CTAs, experimentation, etc.

By closing our book with reference to the cultural dimensions, we assert that you can begin to experiment in your company with the aim of changing the culture – but start small, experiment and don't be put off if it doesn't work the first time around. Just see it as a learning experimentation (with hypotheses similar to what we developed in the exploration phases and a performance dashboard, noting your key learnings) and don't forget to monitor your progress continuously by conducting, interpreting, adjusting and repeating.

Building a portfolio, embracing radical innovations and developing a coherent innovation management portfolio, within a supportive organisational culture takes time and effort but the challenge is worth taking – don't give up! «

ARCHIMEDES SCREW

Creating an innovative organisation can seem like pushing water up hill – but the "Archimedes Screw" made that activity all the more achievable and we believe organising your innovation and establishing the right structure are like engaging that "Archimedes Screw", but remember not all structure work all the time – it is about selecting the right one for the particular radical innovation you have in your sights.

» **Anyone who has never made a mistake has never tried anything new.** «

ALBERT EINSTEIN

ACKNOWLEDGE-MENTS

The authors would like to express our gratitude to all our academic colleagues, companies and students who we have collaborated with and who helped us shape our thinking. In particular, we would like to thank ISPIM Directors Steffen Conn and Iain Bitran for supporting the idea of the Special Interest Group (SIG) on skills and methods for practitioners in innovation management. This group was our starting point to try out and test some of our canvases with practitioners and academics. Olga also thanks her former colleagues from an innovation start-up consultancy, Stim, where she was involved in a variety of consultancy and training projects with large Fortune 500 organisations and managed an Innovation Studio established in 2015 to connect leaders from different organisations such as RATP, Schneider Electric, Turbomeca, Renault, Thales, TechnipFMC, SafranGroup, Valeo to learn, share and act together to improve their innovation practices. It is thanks to her work at Stim and the ISPIM SIG that the idea of the playbook was born.

The views and opinions expressed in this book are those of the authors and do not necessarily reflect the views of our collaborating organisations and colleagues, some of whom we have mentioned.

OLGA KOKSHAGINA   ALLEN ALEXANDER

ABOUT THE AUTHORS

OLGA KOKSHAGINA

STAY IN TOUCH

Olga.Kokshagina@rmit.edu.au

Olga Kokshagina is an innovation practitioner, researcher and advocate for open science and entrepreneurship. She is an assistant professor, lecturer at RMIT University in Australia and she is affiliated with Mines ParisTech PSL Research university in France. She holds a PhD in management science from Mines ParisTech PSL Research University. Her research was a part of an industrial program conducted in collaboration with STMicroelectronics where she was deeply engaged in a range of innovative projects. She co-leads ISPIM special interest group on methods and skills for innovation management practitioners and researchers. Olga is a hub leader for the Melbourne chapter of OneHealthTech grassroots community that aims for a better inclusion in healthtech and co-director of RMIT W+SN network (Wearables and Sensing). Her work focusses on several areas: strategic management of design, open and radical innovation and entrepreneurship. She holds several patents and her work has been published in the leading technology and innovation management journals.

STAY IN TOUCH
A.T.Alexander@exeter.ac.uk

ALLEN
ALEXANDER

Allen Alexander is a senior researcher, who adopts an impact-orientated and practical perspective to his academic studies. He has led many research projects focussed on innovation and entrepreneurship and delivered educational and business support projects that have supported SMEs and MNEs in the UK, Europe and North America. Employed as a senior lecturer at the University of Exeter Business School, his research is published in some of the world's leading peer-reviewed innovation journals. He has also consulted and re-viewed for the UK's Department of Business, Energy and Industrial Strategy, the European Commission H2020 programme and the European Institute for Innovation and Technology as well as being a member of Innovate UK's Innovation Caucus. He is a recipient of the ISPIM Global Innovation Fellowship and Peter Pribilla-Stiftung Leading Innovation Fellowship and previously, chair of the board of directors of the Exeter Science Park and Innovation Centre's operating company. His PhD was focussed on knowledge as a source of innovation and his most recent empirical studies explore circular innovations and the role that they can play in the transition to a circular economy.

ISBN 978-3-11-064129-5
e-ISBN (PDF) 978-3-11-064150-9

Library of Congress Control Number: 2020940472

Bibliographic information published by the Deutsche Nationalbibliothek
The Deutsche Nationalbibliothek lists this publication in the Deutsche
Nationalbibliografie; detailed bibliographic data are available on the internet
at http://dnb.dnb.de.

© 2020 Walter de Gruyter GmbH, Berlin/Boston
Design, Illustration and Typesetting: Editienne, Berlin
Printing and Binding: optimal media GmbH, Röbel

www.degruyter.com